CASTLES IN SPAIN

CASTLES IN SPAIN

PHOTOGRAPHS BY

REINHART WOLF

TEXT BY FERNANDO CHUECA GOITIA

ABBEVILLE PRESS · PUBLISHERS · NEW YORK

*This book is dedicated to the photographer José Ortiz Echagüe.
Through his work I became acquainted with the spirit of Spain;
his footsteps I frequently followed in my search for the castles
of his country.* —Reinhart Wolf

On the jacket (front):
Almansa, at Albacete
See plate 10 (pp. 33–4)

On the jacket (back):
Guadamur, at Toledo
See plate 18 (p. 57)

Library of Congress Cataloging in Publication Data

Chueca Goitia, Fernando.
    Castles in Spain.

    Translation of: De España.
    1. Castles—Spain.   I. Wolf, Reinhart, 1930–
II. Title.
NA7775.C4813   1983   779'.44'0924   83–7267
ISBN 0-89659-390-8

CASTLES IN SPAIN

1. MOYA (Cuenca)
2. CONSUEGRA (Toledo)
3. SÁDABA (Zaragoza)
4. MOMBELTRÁN (Ávila)
5. ATIENZA (Guadalajara)
6. PUENTE DEL CONGOSTO (Salamanca)
7. CASTROGERIZ (Burgos)
8. ALMODÓVAR DEL RÍO (Córdoba)
9. VALENCIA DE DON JUAN (León)
10. ALMANSA (Albacete)
11. CALATAYUD (Zaragoza)
12. VÉLEZ BLANCO (Almería)
13. BELALCÁZAR (Córdoba)
14. MONTEMAYOR DEL RÍO (Salamanca)
15. EMBID (Guadalajara)
16. MONASTERIO DE RODILLA (Burgos)
17. MONTEALEGRE (Valladolid)
18. GUADAMUR (Toledo)
19. TRUJILLO (Cáceres)
20. MEQUINENZA (Zaragoza)
21. JADRAQUE (Guadalajara)
22. LA CALAHORRA (Granada)
23. BELMONTE (Cuenca)
24 NOGALES (Badajoz)
25. PEÑAFIEL (Valladolid)
26. LOARRE (Huesca)
27. BERLANGA DE DUERO (Soria)
28. BARCO DE ÁVILA (Ávila)
29. COCA (Segovia)
30. LA IRUELA (Jaén)
31. MOLINA DE ARAGÓN (Guadalajara)
32. ISCAR (Valladolid)

IT is difficult to introduce this beautiful book of photographs by Reinhart Wolf. I do not know Reinhart Wolf, but his photographs reveal something of his attitudes and his aesthetic sensibility. The realistic depiction of forms or landscapes reveals a spirit easily moved by the grandeur of spectacle. And it is spectacle that the hulking monster of a castle presents in its almost always desolate Castilian landscape. ''The cathedral and the castle,'' said Ortega y Gasset, ''are at once nature and history. They seem natural outcroppings of the rocky farmland, and, at the same time, their purposeful contours possess human meaning. Because of them the landscape intensifies and becomes a stage. The stone, ever strong, is charged with electric spiritual drama.'' These words could have been written as a prologue to this book.

Certainly the castle intensifies the landscape and converts it to a stage; each of Wolf's photographs is proof of this. The castle is a point—sometimes materially so—on an enormous plain with distant horizons, but it colors its surroundings and gives us the key to understanding it, of putting in perspective its relationship to the cosmos. The castle highlights and humanizes the land, for in its powerful presence it is something deeply human. The desolate, deserted, and empty countryside is ignited, however unlikely it may seem, by the rocky flame of a sunburned fortress.

Castle ruins, like the residue of a lost civilization, project a human light, like those stars, dead for thousands of years, that still shine in the heavens. In these superhuman landscapes the castle is often something akin to an insignificant accident amidst the desert or jagged rock; but its very insignificance explains the rest. Just study the photographs of Castrogeriz (plate no. 7), Atienza (plate no. 5), Mequinenza (plate no. 20), and others to see this clearly. There is yet another point. The artist scrupulously avoided the human form, and with that, any animal that might accompany him; and any device, instrument, or tool that might bring man to mind. Not a cart, nor a plow, nor a thresher is evident. All of these, in the mind of the photographer, would trivialize the image and endow it with anecdotal features that would destroy its essential gravity. The human aspect is the castle itself in its unrelieved solitude.

In Wolf's pictures, the castle and its surroundings come together in such a way that they begin to meld, and one cannot tell when the castle has become nature or when the rocky crests and the limestone strata have become walls. In the case of Almansa (plate no. 10), the rock surfaces, folded in such a way as to have become vertical faces, are continued in the castle walls so that it is difficult to distinguish between the two. At Atienza (plate no. 5), the hillocks of sedimentary land seem shaped by the hand of a rough military engineer.

The erosion of the castles is in direct proportion to their ruin, and the advanced decay of the majority of Spanish castles is well known. The word "ruin" comes from the Latin *ruere*, meaning "to fall," and thus it is equivalent to crumbling. A ruin is, therefore, not static but in a state of constant decay. The less intact a building is, the more it seems like nature. Some erosive agents are rain, snow, and the brutal heat of summer. Gentler and more romantic is plant erosion; the combined effect of climbing plants like ivy, bougainvillea, jasmine, honeysuckle, or the more modest hedge mustard, lichen, and fungus. In the dry heartland of Spain, however, this erosion is quite uncommon, and for this, as well as other reasons, the ruins of castles in England are different from those in Spain, which might seem like the *ribats* of the Mogreb or the fortresses of Syria or Mesopotamia. Maurice Legendre tells us that the landscape of Castile is austere and magnificent, barren, yet filled with God. Chateaubriand, well before Renan, likened it to Judea, a monotheistic landscape.

In Wolf's images one rarely sees trees, even though in the beautiful scene of the castle of La Iruela (plate no. 30), in the mountainous region of Jaén, the land is sprinkled with the ash-green dots of olive trees, reminding us of the tassels on a Spanish mantilla. And on the small mountain pedestal where the castle of Jadraque (plate no. 21) sits are sick, dusty, and stunted olive trees that seem to shout their thirst in the white and sunburnt land. The stubborn presence of the evergreen oak could not fail to appear in some of the photographs as it is emblematic of a country of great plains.

But Reinhart Wolf prefers the flatlands, whose dramatic landscape moves him, or the hill country where brush, thyme, and rosemary preserve a delicate and spare greenery. The photographer also makes use of bare winter trees, awakening feelings of cold, anguish, and death. Leafless trees are mere frameworks for foliage, such as those seen at the castle of Montemayor del Río (plate no. 14) and the row of naked trees at the castle of Berlanga de Duero (plate no. 27).

Equally moving are the skies. It has been said that Spain is a land of more sky than earth, that the earth is soaked with heaven's light. In the words of Unamuno:

> *You raise me up, Castile,*
> *In the rugged palm of your hand,*
> *To the heaven that lights and refreshes you,*
> *To the heaven, your lord.*

Wolf has managed to capture this perfectly. He has rendered splendid, dramatic skies, similar to El Greco's. These skies may have always seemed the result of the painter's genius, but they are not entirely so, since those who know Toledo well have often seen them on stormy days when leaden blue clouds are broken by shining breaches.

The sky of Molina de Aragón is splendid and intense, and its blue contrasts with the brown of the land. Another Greco-like sky is found at Sádaba (plate no. 3). The immense sky at Loarre (plate no. 26), mixing its blues with those of the distant Aragonese plain, is pierced by the red, bloodlike brushstrokes of the rays of the setting sun. The rocky profile of the castle emerges, gigantic and solemn on its stone altar, in a stunning silhouette.

Another gorgeous sunset spreads across the landscape of the castle of Iscar (plate no. 32) in Valladolid, while at Coca (plate no. 29) we are witness to a truly disconcerting spectacle. A fantasy castle—the product of a feudal lord's sinful impulse—sculpted with a thousand facets like a fiery opal, gathers the evening light and reverberates against a stormy dark blue sky. If the famous phrase *châteaux en Espagne* makes any sense at all, it is here in this magical castle, so fantastic that it seems unreal, a dream. *Châteaux en Espagne*, the epitome of the impossible. The celestial blue that forms a halo above the castle of Montealegre (plate no. 17) makes its structure more ghostly, its walls pale like a specter's tunic, and its edges knifelike.

Considering the skies, one must, of course, speak of Wolf's use of light. He is a wise manipulator of light, preferring almost always the horizontal light of dawn or dusk. Both sky and light are accented by an intelligent use of filters that highlights the contrasts between the two. When the afternoon light bathes the hard stones in its rays, it ennobles them and turns their harsh surfaces, for a few moments, into an explosion of the purest gold.

The castle of Vélez Blanco (plate no. 12) is a ship of gold sailing into evening; Belalcázar (plate no. 13), a gilded peak among ashen olive trees; Almodóvar del Rio (plate no. 8), the luxurious citadel of an Armenian prince; Nogales (plate no. 24), the crown of a golden oak; Moya (plate no. 1), a dusty ruin with headless towers, warmed by the sun; Berlanga de Duero (plate no. 27), a delicate yellow-green tremor of ocher; La Calahorra (plate no. 22) and Barco de Avila (plate no. 28) exhibit exquisite groupings of ocher, mauve, and snowy white. At Calahorra the light at dusk molds the roundness of the towers set in a landscape of violet tones. At Barco de Avila an entire wall of the fortress absorbs the warm light of the sun while the Gredos mountains display their cold, snowy surfaces, delicately ridged by snowdrifts.

What criteria has Reinhart Wolf used to choose these particular castles? Without a doubt, purely subjective and emotional criteria, at times lyrical and at others dramatic. Ignoring altogether historical importance, architectural uniqueness, chronological sequence, and geographic location during

1.   MOYA (Cuenca)

2. CONSUEGRA (Toledo)

his travels, those castles that stimulated intense emotion are the ones he chose. He searched out the lonely castles, those that rose out of an inhuman, almost timeless emptiness. As Ortega y Gasset says: "Each one brings with it its own setting, always excessive, spectral, somnambulant." It would appear that Wolf read Ortega, for no castle is without its particular landscape, and each has its own posture. They are an outsized and aggressive race, petrified, seemingly, as punishment for their warlike excesses. Wolf also tended towards those castles located in the arid regions of Spain, the desert and plains areas, avoiding the humid and luxuriant sections of the country.

In his photographs there are no castles from Galicia, Cantabria, northern León, northern Burgos, or Catalonia. His are the more severe and haughty castles, those tough highland castles of the two Castiles—of Aragón, of the severe lands of Extremadura; even those of Andalucía are chosen, although for their romantic and picturesque aspects. Naturally, the Castiles own the day: twelve are from Castile and León, and eight from New Castile (which might be confused with the ancient realm of Toledo). Five are from Andalucía, four from Aragón, and three from Extremadura.

Reinhart Wolf naturally did not come looking for images reminiscent of a green Europe, with her well-preserved and polished castles, converted to princely residences, surrounded by gardens, and whose dungeons are reflected in the green-black waters of their moats. He came moved by the flavor of the stronger and stranger dishes that a traveler finds when he crosses the Pyrenees. The dark Spain of Verhaeren or Solana emerges at every corner on the old dusty roads of Castile or Aragón—in a decrepit town submerged in misery; in the cavernous interior of a church where a haggard and bloody Christ shudders, and makes us shudder, by the light of an oil lamp; in the brutal village bullfights, in the black costumes of so many aged fifty-year-olds whose features, lined with deep wrinkles, seem to rise from the very land they inhabit.

From the middle of this landscape, like a pinnacle, surges the castle or what was once the castle; the ruin at once vanquished and proud that keeps among its stones a murmur of history. This ruin is also a part of the dramatic Spain that is such a magnet to foreign artists who arrive here from other lands where life and habitat are so very different from that in Spain. Among those who have fallen under the dark, dramatic spell of the Castilian landscape and her still-defiant castles, must henceforth be counted Reinhart Wolf.

SPAIN is a land of castles. Its central political region is, indeed, called Castile, and takes its name from those fortresses that during the Middle Ages gave it a strong and heroic profile. Throughout Spain castles abound and bear witness to its tumultuous history, especially its medieval history. They are the milestones marking the tides of invasions, they are the witnesses testifying to the height and breadth of the floods by which peoples, tribes, phalanxes—civilizations, in sum—rushed into Spain.

The castle is the symbol of the warrior or the individualistic spirit, as Ortega y Gasset defined it in his renowned essay, *Ideas of the Castles*. The illustrious thinker says that they are also a symbol of the liberal spirit, and that regardless of their warlike character, in them is rooted the defense of the individual against the collective. Ortega writes, "In an earlier time the castles seemed to us a symptom of a life completely unlike our own. We fled from them and sought refuge in the ancient democracies as if they were more attuned to our forms of public life—that of the State. Yet, as we hoped to see ourselves citizens in the style of an Athenian or a Roman, we discovered in ourselves a strange reluctance. The ancient State consumes its members completely, leaving nothing for private life. In the hidden roots of our personality that total dissolution of the individual in the collective of the Polis or Civitas repels us. We are obviously not the pure and completely unique citizens as the flaming oratory of public meetings and editorials claim us to be.

"And suddenly, beyond their theatrical gestures, the castles seem to reveal a treasure-trove of inspirations which coincide exactly with our most profound selves. Their towers are raised to defend the person against the State. Gentleman: long live liberty!"

But not all Spanish castles claim Germanic heritage, and, for reasons obvious in Spanish history, there abound fascinating fortresses from the Islamic world, which, of course, is not so in other Western countries. Islamic culture has bequeathed to Spain not only castles like the impenetrable fortress of Gorman in the province of Soria, the old citadels of Málaga and Granada, and the Aljafería of Zaragoza, but also an important series of enclosures, or walled defensive systems. The walls of the castles at Cáceres and Badajoz, for example, are truly extraordinary constructions with a multitude of innovations such as polygonal towers and *albarrana* (from the Arabic word *barrani*, meaning bachelor) towers which are separate from but connected to the wall proper by an elevated bridge.

Many Moorish castles were later greatly altered

by the Christians and often not just once but repeatedly over the centuries. It is rare to find castles that were built in one continuous effort and can therefore be easily and precisely dated. The majority do not have a fixed date of construction, just as a city has no fixed date except perhaps that of its founding. Thus, with the passage of time, castles continued to be built and taken apart, especially the Moorish ones that, by dint of their age, were the objects of numerous restorations, enlargements, and changes. Castles like that of Alcalá de Guadaira in Sevilla are Moorish in origin, basic structure, and military contrivances, although they may have Roman antecedents. After the region was conquered by Ferdinand III, important alterations were carried out around the year 1424 and between the years 1470 and 1477. This important castle serves, then, as an example of the history of all the castles in Spain: Roman origins, rebuilt by the Almohad Moors, taken by Ferdinand III, and reworked during the fifteenth century.

Other typically Moorish castles like El Conventual of Córdoba, a caliphal fortress, or the castle of San Romualdo in San Fernando (Cádiz) confront us with a world very different from the Western and Germanic one. In fact, the relatively well-preserved castle of San Romualdo may be the one fortress in the peninsula totally reminiscent of Islamic architecture, being a copy of a *ribat*—an Islamic conventual headquarters.

The ideas and advancements in fortification material that the Moors brought to Spain had a powerful influence on the military architecture of the Middle Ages. It was due to Islamic tradition that *mudéjar* castles were unique examples, including those of Medina del Campo and Coca (plate no. 29) in Castile, and those of Malpica, Montalbán, and Escalona in the province of Toledo. Among the buildings constructed in the Western Gothic style, especially those corresponding to the Alcázar de Segovia or to the castles of Olite and Tafalla, there can be found interiors completely decorated in the *mudéjar* style. Many of these decorations have disappeared and only slight vestiges remain of others. For example, in the Salón del Solio at Alcázar de Segovia can be seen the marvelous work of the Moor, Xalel Alcalde—a magnificent tile dado and a grand stucco frieze composed of wide bands that formed a huge loop, covered with a carved wooden dome.

Using only the Spanish castles as examples, one could illustrate the entire history of fortification during the Middle Ages with supremely typical characteristics. In the oldest castles, from the thirteenth and fourteenth centuries, the architectural forms were more elemental, basic. They stood out because of their magnificence, their great prismatic forms, and sheer volume. The towers, for example,

3.   SÁDABA (Zaragoza)

4. MOMBELTRÁN (Ávila)

5. ATIENZA (Guadalajara)

had smooth flat exteriors without the rows of machicolations that later enlivened the profiles of castles at the end of the fourteenth century and the beginning of the fifteenth century. These towers, which were either geometric or cylindrical in shape, were crowned by battlements that in many cases were destroyed due to their fragility, leaving the tops of the walls resembling nicked and ragged rows of teeth. Examples of this powerful dimensionality can be found in the castles of Molina de Aragón (plate no. 31); Montealegre (plate no. 17); Medina de Pomar in the province of Burgos, with its two immense, enormously forceful towers; and Almansa (plate no. 10).

Many of these strong, elemental castles complete the silhouette of the steep, rocky promontories upon which they sit, becoming one with nature in a surprising way. This is the case with the rock castles that are so abundant in Spain: Loarre (plate no. 26), the Alcázar de Segovia, Montearagón, Albuquerque (Badajoz), and, above all, Almansa in the province of Albacete.

After this, castles became richer and more complicated in design, and there developed what could be called a peculiar style—the castle aesthetic. Elements that were originally defensive in character were converted, without losing their original function, into emblematic and even decorative forms.

This change occurred not only as a natural evolution, but also because the great lords of the Castilian, Aragonese, and Andaulusian nobility sought to show their power and secure their estates with these fortresses and to impress with their luxury and magnificence. Castles such as Coca (plate no. 29), built by the Fonseca family, should not be seen simply as military strongholds, but rather as fortified palaces that proclaimed the wealth and magnificence of their owners. This occurred, to a greater or lesser degree, with all the castles built during the fourteenth and fifteenth centuries. The principal tower or "tower of homage" of the Alcázar de Segovia, from the era of John II, is a magnificent example of this type of architecture—part military and part lordly—and of this type of aesthetic. The powerful machicolated gallery, formed of brackets, supporting a series of small arches which in turn supported the battlements; the ornate conical squinches; the machicolations turned into decorative canopies with loopholes; and the typically Segovian *graffito* give this tower a lordly appearance. Castles such as those of Peñafiel (plate no. 25), Fuensaldaña, and Torrelobatón in Valladolid; Galve in Guadalajara; Alarcón in Cuenca; Pambre in Lugo; Olite in Navarra; Oropesa in Toledo; Belmonte de Campos in Valencia; and many others with towers lacking the beauty of the tower of the Segovian Alcázar share the same aesthetic. Particularly outstanding among them are the principal towers with their multiple turrets and their finely worked machicolations and battlements. The renowned castle of Medina del Campo, the frequent residence of Queen Isabella, with its elegant principal tower, is actually in this style. Because this castle was built with brick, however, it can also be considered *mudéjar* in style, even though it follows the forms of the Gothic castle.

At the end of the fifteenth century, and with the appearance of firearms (especially artillery), castle design changed noticeably: its profile, indeed its very aesthetic, took on different features. The castle became less elevated, being built closer to the ground, and strong banked walls appeared. A typical sixteenth-century castle—built low, spread out, and with thick banked walls—is the one at Grajal de Campos in the province of León. Another typical artillery castle is the famous castle of La Calahorra (plate no. 22) in Granada. On the other hand, the castle-palace of the House of Albuquerque in Cuéllar, Segovia, has a mixed design, still maintaining many of the more traditional characteristics.

At the very end of the fifteenth century and during the sixteenth, the castle-palace makes a dramatic appearance. Earlier there had been purely military castles, which had within their interiors richly adorned rooms, generally decorated in Gothic or *mudéjar* motifs, but they were not, properly speaking, castle-palaces; they were castles with luxury apartments inside. The castle-palace is another thing entirely and is planed and conceived as such. One of the most renowned castle-palaces that exists in Spain is at Manzanares el Real in the province of Madrid, the property of the Palace of Infantado and the work of the late, great Gothic architect Juan Guas. It is a true palace within a well-planned military shell, with high battlement walls, cylindrical towers, and graceful *caballeros*. When a tower of large diameter is extended by another smaller tower on top, this smaller one is called a *caballero*, no doubt because it rides the larger tower like a knight. The rich exterior decoration and the splendid Isabelline patio of the castle at Manzanares el Real create a truly palatial appearance. Some of the more famous castle-palaces are those at Cuéllar, Belmonte (plate no. 23) in Cuenca, Grajal de Campos in León, Zafra in Badajoz, Vélez Blanco (plate no. 12) in Almería, Calahorra (plate no. 22) in Granada, Canena in Jaén, Simancas in Valladolid, and Villaviciosa de Odón in Madrid. The Arabic form of the castle-palace is known as the *alcazaba*, of which more shall be said when Andalucía is discussed.

Castle-palaces usually had a more regular and geometric floor plan, having been designed with a single function in mind. Generally, the layout is more or less rectangular or square with circular towers at the corners, and the nucleus of the fortress is made up of a principal courtyard, which in some cases is a great architectural work in itself. For example, the courtyards at Manzanares el Real, at Calahorra (plate no. 22), or at Vélez Blanco (plate no. 12) in Almería may be considered major works of Isabelline or Plateresque architecture. Also worthy of note are the courtyards at Cuéllar, Villa-nueva de Cañedo in Salamanca, and Canena in Jaén.

As for the organization and layout of castles in general, and excluding these special cases, there were no fixed rules or consistent typologies. The plans often tended to be irregular because they were adapted to the existing conditions of the terrain: the ridges, hillocks, summits, and abrupt scarps where they were usually built. In the case of the rock castles, the curtains or sheets of walls stretch and bend to suit this landscape. One of the prime examples of this style is the castle of Peñafiel (plate no. 25) in Valladolid, which molds itself to a ridge forming a long, thin ship. Similarly the castle of Zorita de los Canes in Guadalajara and many other castles have adapted to their settings in this way.

In a sort of progression, a row of walls, or barbicans, is usually followed by the main walls that enclose the central keep of the castle. Generally the principal tower, which was the fundamental bastion and last redoubt of the fortress in case of siege, is mounted on the wall. Rarely was it placed in the center of the keep, to avoid its being surrounded should the walls have been stormed and taken. Often the principal tower is also found in a corner, and the variety of large and small towers, defensive and connecting walls, walkways, ditches, and barbicans is infinite. Only a few military castles of a later period, such as those of Fuensaldaña, Torrelobatón, Ampudia, or Montealegre (plate no. 17), display any kind of symmetry and order without sacrificing their principal military characteristics.

It has already been said that Spain is a land of castles, and that their number, in spite of numerous destructions, is enormous. A map issued by the Dirección General de Bellas Artes some years ago, listed 2,538 castles, fortresses, towers, and walled areas. It should also be remembered that in 1456 Henry IV destroyed many castles belonging to the nobility because of their potential threat to royal power. The same precaution was later taken by the Catholic kings and even Cardinal Cisneros. Yet the impressive number, 2,538, still remains.

It is evident, as we have already mentioned, that the great majority of Spanish castles are in ruins, and some are so dilapidated that their walls and towers remain like desperate survivors awaiting their final destruction.

Don Antonio Ponz, the illustrious and enlight-

6. PUENTE DEL CONGOSTO (Salamanca)

7.   CASTROGERIZ (Burgos)

8. ALMODÓVAR DEL RÍO (Córdoba)

ened eighteenth-century traveler, commented that "one of the most pitiable desertions that I find wherever I travel in Spain is that of these forts and castles, whose honorable appearance gave to their towns and cities (since almost all had them) an air of majesty. If they had only been left alone these castles, built five or six centuries ago, would still be standing."

The ruin of these castles has accelerated, and only recently have these national treasures begun to attract interest. Some may say that the ruins are far more romantic and moving than the restored edifices, and perhaps Reinhart Wolf was seduced by the fierce appearance of these castle ruins and their suggestion of vanquished warriors imploring pardon for their ancient excesses. Nevertheless, if the decay continues, there may come a time when even these noble vestiges will disappear. Fortunately, these fortresses are receiving ever more care and attention from the authorities, public and private associations, and architects dedicated to their restoration.

In France and Germany military castles were eventually transformed into luxurious, palatial residences. Thus the châteaux of the Loire maintained their vitality while shedding their warlike gear of yesteryear to assume the dressings and adornments of the cheery Renaissance architecture. The same has happened to the Rhine castles. They are well preserved and maintained as luxurious residences with their full profiles and multiple towers uplifted by their conical roofs. Of all this, Spain has only the Alcázar de Segovia, which seems today more a European castle than one of the battered giants that abound in the country.

Moreover, just as castles have neither age nor date of birth, neither do they have known creators. Built and rebuilt over time, not only by different men but by different civilizations, those who designed these repeatedly destroyed and rebuilt fortresses remain unknown. At times it seems as absurd to wonder who planned them as it is to wonder who made the hills where they stand.

Only at the very end of the fifteenth century do creators emerge from the anonymity of the old stone workers. The castle of Manzanares el Real of the Mendoza family had a well-known designer: the same architect who built the Palace of Infantado in Guadalajara for this noble family. And, curiously, the castle is fitted out in fancy dress like a palace while the palace itself includes the military architecture of a castle. Juan Guas, the designer of these two distinguished works, transferred forms from one to the other. There is no doubt that the Renaissance palace is, in its early stages, a likeness of the medieval castle, just as the automobile was of the horse-drawn carriage. The castle aesthetic greatly influenced the morphology of the

Renaissance palace, and this can be seen in the origins of both Florentine and French palaces. In fact the word "palace" in French was absorbed by the word *chateau*. In Spain the same thing occurred, although in its own unique way.

This is not the place to embark on a critical study and architectural analysis. Suffice it to say the castle had its own aesthetic and played a preponderant role when the military needs that originally dictated its forms had long since disappeared. It is true that form follows function—the maxim that appealed so strongly to rationalist architects—but it must also be remembered that form, once created, is freed from function and can live without it. Battlements, machicolations, crenellations, and a variety of towers, lookouts, and turrets were born of the demands of war but went on to live independently as symbols or emblems of lineage or power. The castle aesthetic is, after all, the heritage of noble lords, and when these nobles deserted their towers and castles in the country for the city, they brought with them their own artistic forms.

CASTLES IN CASTILE

IN Castile there is a castle, it is called Rocha Frida. . . ." So goes the old ballad. But everyone knows that there are many in this land, the very heart and soul of Spain. What is more, the land itself is like a castle. In the lapidary phrase of Don Salvador de Madariaga, "The essential fact about the Spanish land is its inaccessability; Spain is a castle." A little later in his book, *Spain, An Essay of Contemporary History*, he continues: "The citadel of this castle is the Central Plateau, a geographic formation that covers more than two-thirds of the territory at an average altitude of 700 meters. . . . This plateau gives the country its typical traits: elevation, emptiness, space. . . . Elevated, bare, and spacious, this Spain imprints on the spirit a profound feeling of primitive force, whether in the summer when it receives over its monkish cloak the ardent caress of a cruel sun; in the autumn, when the deep purple clouds drag their mysterious shadows in the silence of its unlimited plains; in the bright winter when it seems as if the sun's light lends its cold reflections to the sharp knives of the mountain winds; or in the fugitive spring. The Castilian plateau is a country of grandeur, worthy companion to the great natural essences—sea and sky—and to the great states of the spirit—poetry and contemplation."

It is evident that in this rough and untamed land the castle is a mythical but essential personage who explains and makes meaningful a warlike and on many occasions dramatic landscape. Sometimes the nude and barren countryside, upon which the naked skeleton of the castle bleaches like the jawbone of an antediluvian animal, reminds us of José Hierros's lines:

This plain of death, this accursed land,
This naked hillock of parched flanks,
This sad wasteland, where the shouts of man
Find not a mountain to return its echoes,
This desert world, this life so dull,
This solitude like an ocher skull.

Also skull-like are the castles, with their empty hollow eyes and their bleached white teeth. They are many, these castles of Castile, and the region possesses some of the finest examples, such as Gormaz, Peñafiel (plate no. 25), Fuensaldaña, Coca (plate no. 29), Torrelobatón (Cúellar), Segovia, Turegano. . . . Valladolid is a particularly castled province. Although Wolf does not claim to have chosen castles for their antiquity, architectural importance, or historical ancestry alone, he did include more castles from Old Castile than those of any other region in Spain. Within Castile, the province of Valladolid attracts the most attention, and Wolf includes the castles of Peñafiel, Iscar (plate no. 32), and Montealegre (plate no. 17).

From the province of Burgos, Wolf has chosen the castle of Castrogeriz (plate no. 7) and the Monasterio de Rodilla (plate no. 16); from Segovia, Coca (plate no. 29); from Soria, Berlanga de Duero (plate no. 27); from León, Valencia de Don Juan (plate no. 9); from Ávila, the castles of Mombeltrán (plate no. 4) and Ávila; and finally, from Salamanca, those of Puente de Congosto (plate no. 6) and Montemayor del Río (plate no. 14).

Beginning with the Valladolid castles, the first to be discussed is the illustrious castle at Peñafiel.

Peñafiel (plate no. 25) is one of the jewels of Spanish military architecture, rising between the rivers Duero and Duratón in a countryside full of Castilian history that reminds us of the marquis of Loyola's verses:

Roads of Segovia, of Olmedo and Tordesillas
Paths of Peñafiel, of Roa and of Ontiveros;
Beneath the dust's face, kneeling I seek
the footprints of saints and of knights.

The ridge on which the the castle sits is itself in the form of a ship, a ready metaphor for the castle that follows its lines. As the count of Gamazo says, ''The imagination of a biblical reader would see in it a rocky imitation of Noah's Ark stranded on the summit of Mount Ararat.''

The castle, with an enormous principal tower, and one of the finest in Castile, in its center, its extensive length and meager breadth appears to be

9. VALENCIA DE DON JUAN (León)

10. ALMANSA (Albacete)

11. CALATAYUD (Zaragoza)

a battleship of solid rigging unscathed by time.

This site was conquered in the eleventh century by Count Sancho García and ceded by Alfonso X to his brother, Prince Don Juan Manuel, who, beginning in 1307, enlarged an old fortress that had been dismantled in 1294. The principal tower was rebuilt during the time of John II and is a fine summation of fifteenth-century aesthetics. The wall measures 820 feet long and 95 feet wide. Reinforcing the parapet are thirty circular towers reached by stone steps, some of which are covered with spherical vaults. Did the author of *El Conde Lucanor* climb them? The great historical and literary figure Prince Don Juan Manuel, great-grandson of Ferdinand the Saint, was master of these lands and this castle, now a hollow coffer signifying the power of yesteryear.

"On the top of a hill, almost midpoint between the roads of Olmedo and Cuéllar, as if grabbing the bald prominence to keep from crashing down, can be seen the remains of the castle of Iscar, over which still arises, elegant and swaggering with its old coat of arms, the quadrangular homage tower."—Gamazo

Noted for its principal tower, the castle of Iscar (plate no. 32) is one of Castile's most graceful and lofty castles. It excels above all because of its solitary hilltop location from which it oversees the plains of the rivers Cega and Eresma. It seems that this area was inhabited by Alvar Fañez de Minaya, nephew and lieutenant of El Cid.

We know neither what stronghold was built then nor what the castle was like when its governor refused entrance to Alfonso XI. The existing tower dates from the fifteenth century and the architecture and the coat of arms, majestically placed high on a wall, correspond to the style of that period.

One could say of Iscar what the poet José Zorilla said about the castle of Fuensaldaña:

From feudal splendor, naked debris
Without tapestries, weapons, or carpets,
Today its muted walls protect
Nothing more than silence, solitude, and shade.
Old tales live on, perhaps,
Under its forgotten name,
And among the vaults, towers, and columns
Sprout forth patches of weeds.
Birds inhabit the roof
And the industrious spider covers it . . .
Enclosing the coarse sorrow
Of the old tower of Fuensaldaña.

Montealegre is near Medina de Rioseco, city of the admirals of Castile, and its neighbors are the magnificent castle of Ampudia and those of Villalba de los Alcores.

The castle of Montealegre (plate no. 17) is pure geometry; its sharp lines and crystalline volume are mitigated by the delicate counterpoint of short circular turrets. It is a castle both confident and fierce—fitted for battle—without the slightest concession to ornamentation. Like so many Spanish castles, it stands alone in the broad Castilian landscape, against a deep sky, scorching in the summer and as sharp as crystal in the winter. Here one may speak of warlike plains and ascetic wastelands.

In the time of Alfonso VIII, Montealegre belonged to the feudal estate of Alfonso Téllez. The Order of Santiago gave the estate jurisdiction and Alfonso the Wise granted it privileges. This was the estate of the House of Albuquerque, elevated to the county of Montealegre in the person of Don Enrique Manuel de Villena. It was later passed on to the House of Guzmán with Philip IV creating the title marquis of Montealegre for Don Martín de Guzmán. In relatively recent times, it has joined with the houses of Ladrón de Guevara, Oñate, and Los Arcos. The title was finally transferred to the ducal House of Nájera.

In the northwest of the province of Segovia, bordering on Valladolid, on a flat land sprinkled with patches of pine groves, is the castle of Coca (plate no. 29), bastion of the powerful Fonseca family and a beautiful mystery of Spanish military architecture. It has no precedents and nothing compares with it. It was constructed by Moorish architects, well versed in the art of brick masonry, but its military design was purely Western, even

modern. It has moats and banks typical of fortresses armed with artillery, as it is a creation from the end of the fifteenth and the beginning of the sixteenth centuries. There may have been an earlier fortress on the site of which only a few remnants of masonry remain.

The castle is almost square in layout with two enclosures, each with large corner towers and smaller towers and lookouts on the walls. Its broad moat, built not for water but for protection from artillery, leaves the bulk of the castle submerged and, from some points of view, renders it less elegant. The principal tower is powerful; embroidered with small towers and cylindrical turrets, it occupies one of the corners in the inner court. In spite of the *mudéjar* clothing, it is perfectly Western and Gothic in concept. In Spain there are many intrinsically Moslem fortresses such as the castles of Montalbán, Malpica, Alcalá de Guadaira, and San Romualdo in San Fernando (Cádiz), not to mention those citadels that are historically Moslem. Stylistically, Coca reminds one of a small chapel in Guadalajara built in a similar spirit, in brick, by Don Luis de Lucena during the sixteenth century.

Don Vicente Lampérez has said that this castle must have been conceived by a great lord and executed by an extravagant goldsmith; it could be compared with Milanese breastplates in which the defensive casing is covered with a splendid layer of damascene and engraving. The great lord was Don Alonso de Fonseca, described by his contemporary, Hernando del Pugar, in *Los claros varones de España*: "A man of very sharp wit . . . who wanted his personal necessities to be most excellent and to have a singularity of perfection over all the others. . . ." We can only imagine what the archbishop of Sevilla, Don Alonso de Fonseca, would have built within the interior of his castle-palace, considering the magnificence of the exterior. Nothing of the interior has survived intact, but the exterior shell is a sufficient guide, well preserved and certainly judiciously restored.

In the most barren and uncultivated part of the province of Burgos, bordering on the Palencian Tierra de Campos, lies Castrogeriz or Castro Sigericum. It is a village on the road to Santiago, interesting for its urban layout, which is typical of the small towns on the pilgrimage route. In the case of Castrogeriz, the hamlet develops linearly, seeking the protection of a hilltop where the ruins of an ancient castle of Visigothic origin remain. Today this castle (plate no. 7) is an almost shapeless ruin.

The Monasterio de Rodilla (plate no. 16) in Burgos, on the site of the medieval frontier between Castile and Navarre, is a sad stump of what was once an important fortress during the battles between the Navarrese and Castilians. Like many others these remains are, in Machado's words, "scattered rags of an old suit of armor." The landscape is desolate and rough, with limestone rocks joining the ruined walls in their desolate solitude.

The province of Soria is blessed with extremely beautiful and historically significant castles, beginning with that of Gormaz, the most important caliphal fortress in all Castile and the defensive bastion of the Duero line, continuing with Almenar, Calatañazor, Monteagudo de las Vicarias, Burgo de Osma, and Magaña. But Wolf has photographed only Berlanga de Duero (plate no. 27), whose massive strength has defied the erosion of time. The fortress consists of an exterior enclosure with many towers, reminiscent of the walls of Ávila, and a modern castle-palace of the sixteenth century that protects a more ancient principal tower.

Incredibly, on this site the dukes of Frias had a luxurious palace and a number of pleasant gardens where the children of Francis I of France could relax during their captivity: *Sic transit gloria mundi*. Ortega y Gasset sees it in this way: "This is the castle of Berlanga, of a silvery color, stretched over a live rock, an immense steep ground of limestone, that from far away shines so brilliantly the whole seems embossed in silver."

Traveling from the dryness of the Castilian plateau to the mountainous foothills of the Sierra de Gredos, we come upon a most pleasant scene. The castle of Mombeltrán (plate no. 4) is set on one of

12. VÉLEZ BLANCO (Almería)

13.   BELALCÁZAR (Córdoba)

14. MONTEMAYOR DEL RÍO (Salamanca)

the most beautiful sites in Spain, the Puerta del Pico mountain pass, on the highway from Toledo to Ávila. It was the feudal estate of Don Beltrán de la Cueva, favorite of Henry IV and presumed father of Juana la Beltraneja. The castle rears up on a small hill, with a background of the lofty and rocky mountains of the Gredos range. It is a unified structure of clear and regular symmetry, pentagonal ground plan, cylindrical towers in the corners, an extremely wide principal tower, also cylindrical, and a superb projecting double-machicolated gallery with granite battlements. The first enclosure has a sharply sloping wall typical of artillery castles. From far away its entire silhouette is reminiscent of an Italian castle. At its foot, old olive trees are proof of the mild and fertile climate in the middle of this wild mountain area. "This is the castle of Mombeltrán, on a valley floor below Gredos, totally exquisite, marked by roundness, watching over the valley where the five villages of Mombeltrán lie" (Ortega).

The village of Barco de Ávila is located in a highland valley on the river Tormes, behind the bulk of the Sierra de la Nava, in the center of the Gredos chain. It was an important site from which cattle passes between the two Castilian plateaus could be guarded. Cool and pleasing woodlands abound here, and the almost perpetual snows of the Gredos peaks assure fertility and good pastures.

The castle (plate no. 28) is not architecturally significant: simply a quadrangle with solid cylindrical towers at its corners and a rectangular, oblong principal tower set over one of its walls. Since it has lost its machicolations and crests, it has remained gloomy and naked, silently hovering over the land and protecting the nearby town of Valdecorneja.

If the provinces of Santander, Burgos, Logroño, Valladolid, Soria, Ávila, and Segovia until recently belonged officially to Old Castile, those of León, Zamora, Palencia, and Salamanca composed the Kingdom of León. Of the castles that appear in this book, one castle is from the province of León and two are from Salamanca.

The castle of Valencia de Don Juan (plate no. 9) in León province, on the edge of the river Esla, is built in a town that bears the name of Valencia de Don Juan in memory of Prince Don Juan, the son of Alfonso X. Yet nothing remains from those times. The fortress whose gaping ruins are contemplated today is entirely from the fifteenth century. When these lands near the Esla were the domain of the counts of Oñate, the castle probably had a splendid silhouette, but perhaps it is more picturesque in ruins than it was intact. The numerous little towers that mark the corners of the principal ring of walls give it the appearance of a stone pipe organ.

Puente de Congosto (plate no. 6) in the province of Salamanca is a good example of a castle defending a bridgehead. It belonged to the ducal House of Alba and is fairly well preserved. The principal tower is so expansive and powerful that it defies time. The river's limestone bed, with its vertical layers whitened by the course of the waters, the solid bridge, and the castle form a solemn ensemble.

Montemayor del Río (plate no. 14) is a perfect Salmantine castle of fine masonry that probably dates from the fourteenth century. It is situated in an attractive and picturesque place not far from Béjar on the frontier between Cáceres and Salamanca.

IN THE KINGDOM OF TOLEDO

THE Spanish region that for administrative reasons has been dubbed New Castile (an ambiguous and to some extent imprecise name) corresponds to what used to be called the Kingdom of Toledo and what is now called, in the new Spain of autonomies, the Castilian-Machegan region. It is preferable to speak of the Kingdom of Toledo, however, since it brings to mind broad historical associations. Toledo was the capital of Spain when the peninsula was controlled by invading Germanic tribes and the Visigoths. Since that time Toledo's great prestige has sprung from her famous religious councils and her outstanding men, like San Ildefonso, Eladio, Justo, Eugenio the Astronomer, and Eugenio the Poet, all archbishops of Toledo and the guiding lights of her councils.

With the Moorish invasion, Toledo declined in importance and Córdoba became the shining star of Spanish cities. But Toledo always remained a myth, having a revered past, a sort of Golden Age for the knights of the Reconquest to regain. And, indeed, Toledo was reconquered quite early, in 1085, during the reign of Alfonso VI, although its occupation was accomplished more through political maneuvering than through siege and conquest. Toledo's star was rekindled then, and the ghost of its kingdom still remains part of the city's legend. But the kingdom was for many reasons subordinated to civil and religious authorities. The Visigothic Toledo of the Councils continues today in Toledo, the city of Spain's Catholic primate. As a result, the diocese of Toledo has attained enormous size, including parts of such Andalusian lands as the present provinces of Jaén and Granada. The territory of the Toledan diocese came to reconstitute the ghostly kingdom mentioned and to some extent that very territory eventually became New Castile, including the vast lands of the military orders ceded by the king to the monastic militias as a reward for their military accomplishments during the Reconquest.

If the city of Toledo seems totally to dominate the entire region, it is because it encapsulates the spirit of the province. The region and the province are possessed, overwhelmed, by Toledo's importance.

Don Manuel Bartolomé Cossio wrote that Toledo is the city that offers the most chracteristic and complete ensemble of all that is truly Spanish in regard to its civilization and its land. It is the most inclusive, brilliant, and suggestive summary of the nation's history. If a traveler had only one day to stay in Spain, he would do best to spend that day in Toledo. Other cities have important monuments, and some are unique—such as the aqueduct of Segovia, the mosque at Córdoba, or Granada's Alhambra—but no city presents so splendid a summation of the typical and unique conditions of a people. This "craggy mass, glory of Spain and light of her cities,' as Cervantes called it, unites the key civilizations of Spanish history. Don Gregorio Marañon said that Toledo, anchored on rough cliffs in the middle of dry Castile is, despite her location, more Mediterranean than all the cities of Greece, Italy, and Spain's eastern shores. Each of these cities on the sunny beaches of a blue sea is part of the immense soul that first endowed the human race with dignity, and even today is its guiding light. But Toledo, far from the sea, is the sum and model of them all.

Toledo is not, as has been claimed, a Castilian city, or perhaps it is only half so. Ávila and Segovia, Burgos and León are purely Castilian. Toledo possesses something that is rather more than Castilian: an oriental character, a Mediterraneanness.

The Imperial City is a crossroads of racial currents, a flask in which the slow flame of centuries has distilled the souls of ancient civilizations; those that came from the barbarous North, those from rough and impetuous Africa, those from the mystic and distant Orient and, even before, those that already occupied the Iberian plateaus when all the others arrived. Still, of all these cultures, whose particular influences are still felt, the strongest is

15.   EMBID (Guadalajara)

16. MONASTERIO DE RODILLA (Burgos)

17. MONTEALEGRE (Valladolid)

from the Mediterranean. Toledo looks from its innermost soul, high on its cliffs, towards the East. The change experienced in the land and the people when crossing the Straits of Gibraltar, is less abrupt than the simple trip to Toledo from Madrid. From the river Manzanares with its hilly lands to the Sagra with its river Tagus, the spiritual distance is a hundred times greater than the short royal highway that connects them.

Toledo is the frontier city of the Mediterranean. It brushes on Castile without entering it. It could be said that Toledo intended to cross Spain and take to the far shores that were once the Land's End of the known world but, exhausted after crossing the rough mountains and endless plains of Castile, it rested on the hills of the Tagus and remained there forever, petrified, held by five immortal spikes, the four spires of the Alcázar and the tower of the cathedral.

To say "Toledo" does not evoke a peaceful image of a world by the sea, as does the name "Cantabria"; nor the opulence of gold on blue at the eastern shores; the grace of Andalusian olive groves dotted with white farms; nor the ferocity of Gredos, of Moncayo, of the Pyrenees, of the Alpujarras, and other Iberian mountains; not even the sea of grain or the hard and melancholy plains of Castile. It evokes none of this, yet it is all of this at once: the symbol of all that is picturesque and glorious woven into the great cape, spread to the sun, that is the Iberian peninsula. This, then, is Toledo, the sum of six superimposed civilizations, an immortal crossroad of cultures, an important link between East and West, a lodging for all the religions of Rome and Spain. This brief name represents the genius of all the poets and historians who worked and polished the Spanish language, as well as the gulleys where for centuries ran the blood of armies fighting for all kinds of ideals and ambitions. But Toledo means more still. Like so many other names of Spanish cities, it was carried on the explorers' ships, in the hearts of those superhuman men dubbed "conquistadors" and who ought to have been called "civilizers" because they did not discover lands to win them, but rather to bring them their civilization. These men left in the New World, among the lasting traces of their presence, the names of distant cities: Córdoba, Trujillo, Mérida, Cartagena, Santiago, Granada, and Toledo, several Toledos, in both North and South America.

The city of Toledo, despite the huge changes in most Spanish cities, has not completely changed. Still to be enjoyed is its timeless atmosphere; still to be experienced are the same sensations Maurice Barrès felt when he wrote The Secret of Toledo and began to realize that the city he was seeing was not very different from one El Greco knew. And if Barrès saw a city like El Greco's, still to be seen is a city like Maurice Barrès's.

Barrès describes Toledo: "In El Greco's time it was the same city I see now; it was the same river that still flows by in front of me. . . . It remains the city on a granite mountain, surrounded by the deep ravine of the Tagus. Amidst an unchanging countryside there is still today a huge climbing cluster of churches, convents, Gothic buildings, and narrow Arabic dwellings. Its stone still murmurs the same words El Greco heard and brought to his paintings. The truths of Toledo! . . . The brilliant dialogue between Christian and Arabic cultures; adversaries once, later indistinguishable!"

Toledo the city is, moreover, like a big castle, a fortified Jerusalem asserting itself on its base with the Tagus as its moat. Even the surrounding countryside is warlike. Ortega y Gasset said that Toledans who go out for a walk on the walls see the nearby hills flex their arms like crossbows ready to fire their arrows in defense. Enemy arrows seem to fly constantly from the surrounding escarpments, recalling ready offensive and defensive systems that today lie dormant but which seem ready to awaken at any moment. Ortega thus saw Toledo as primarily a military city. It certainly was at one time, and to a point it still is. By some arcane mystery it became the site of the oldest and most renowned military academy in Spain. This academy initially occupied the Alcázar, at one time a mighty fortress whose military attributes were softened by the architects of Charles V when they converted it into a palace. It has subsequently been destroyed and rebuilt many times.

The city of Toledo has notable fortifications quite apart from the Alcázar. The castle of San Fernando, the fortified bridges of Alcántara and San Martín, the impressive series of walls and armed gates, towers like the *Hierro* ("Iron") tower, and bridgeheads like the Baño de la Cava tower. Without leaving Toledo's gates, one could study quite thoroughly many chapters concerning Spain's military architecture.

In the province of Toledo, Reinhart Wolf was interested in the castles of Guadamur (plate no. 18), near the capital, and Consuegra (plate no. 2), in the Toledan section of La Mancha; that is to say, that region of La Mancha that covers four provinces: part of Toledo, almost all of Ciudad Real, a bit of Cuenca, and much of Albacete. There are undoubtedly many other outstanding castles in Toledo, among them such important ones as Escalona and Maquede, that once belonged to the powerful Don Alvaro de Luna; Oropesa castle; Malpica castle (which resembles a Moorish fortress); and the castle of Montalbán with the Almohad-inspired military innovations such as its *albarrana* towers. The castle at Barcience is also interesting because its principal tower contains a sculpted relief of a lion reminiscent of Syrian designs.

Reinhart Wolf has also photographed several castles from the province of Guadalajara: Atienza (plate no. 5), Molina de Aragón (plate no. 31), Jadraque (plate no. 21), and Embid (plate no. 15); each one unique in its structure, characteristics, and setting. And, finally, he has included two castles from New Castile: the fortress of Moya (plate no. 1) and the castle-palace of Belmonte (plate no. 23), both in Cuenca.

Of the Toledan castles, Guadamur (plate no. 18), which is only a few miles from the city of Toledo, is a forceful structure because of its rough, ash-colored masonry, and an elegant one because of its stylish profile and numerous small towers. Within the primary enclosure it appears as if one castle is resting upon another. Perhaps the original structure was too low and was later raised. The lower secton of the castle has large circular towers and, rather oddly, some angular towers resembling a bridge's breakwater. The principal tower is impressive in its rectangular mass with its six turrets on projecting arches. Built by Don Pedro López Ayala, the first count of Fuensalida and favorite of John II, after centuries of decay it was rebuilt by the Catalonian count of Asalto.

The castle of Consuegra (plate no. 2) is very different. The novitiate of the military Order of Saint John of Jerusalem, it rests atop a modest ridge that forms a barrier to the winds that blow across the plains of La Mancha. There are windmills located along the ridge, and their whiteness contrasts with the golden ocher of the castle's bastions. The castle is sober and almost unadorned but intelligently laid out, as the men of Saint John sought utility, not beauty. These lands saw difficult times during the Reconquest and the monk/soldiers found these castles safe bases from which to extend their conquests, and they never lacked a chapel in which to invoke their god of war.

Moving on to Guadalajara, which is culturally, artistically, and religiously a continuation of Toledo, there is Atienza (plate no. 5), a stronghold throughout the Duero line. The structure has surrendered to nature; the geometrically stratified limestone hills, formed as rocky bastions, are alone almost enough to create the castle. Man has added very little. Nature's caprice thus produced the predecessor to Coca castle (plate no. 29) before man even existed. A few walls were added in Moorish times and later a square tower that still rises from a rocky edge. In the *Poem of My Cid* the castle was called "a very strong rock [that the] Moors have." Men have time and again coveted this crag as a stronghold in their warring adventures, but while these men and their battles have passed on, the hill persists, smoothed and polished by the rain's greedy kiss; a kiss that never turned the nearby

18.   GUADAMUR (Toledo)

19.   TRUJILLO (Cáceres)

20. MEQUINENZA (Zaragoza)

thirsty meadows green.

The castle at Molina de Aragón (plate no. 31), forms a complete defense system for a city that rests peacefully at its feet. Aben Galván, El Cid's Moorish ally, must have slept soundly knowing he was protected by this fortress. The system included a wall around the city and, on the overlooking hill, a walled enclosure where the city's populace could take refuge. Reinforcing the perimeter of the enclosure at one corner was the castle, with more barbicans, a rectangular enclosure, and six towers, five square and one pentagonal. Finally, on the hilltop was a large simple tower with its own enclosure, which was attached to the main precinct by a strong connecting wall. The single pentagonal tower, named the Tower of Aragón, is quite run down. The group as a whole, however, makes a striking impression, indeed, an oriental image. For although the castle at Molina de Aragón was largely rebuilt in the twelfth and thirteenth centuries, one still sees its ancient Moorish design. The construction, of ocher masonry with red, iron-rich stone blocks at the corners, gives this strictly military edifice a touch of style. The small towers rise up amidst an empty ocher landscape that resembles felt, soft to the touch; the walls and large towers fit into the same scheme. The deep blue sky adds to the coloring its portentous storm clouds.

It seems as though the hillock of Jadraque was arranged by nature's design to be the base for a castle that, however it may have appeared, must have produced an unforgettable impression on travelers. After the ostentatious architecture of the fifteenth century, the castle is again plain, with walls and simple battlement towers. The hillock magnifies and exalts it, even though it may be bleak, with its stained earth and its thirsty olive trees.

Arab chronicles cite a castle planned in 801, to overlook the fertile lowlands of Henares and the approaches to Guadalajara. It must have been a modest construction, and it is not known what remained of it when it was destroyed by Don Pedro Gonzalez de Mendoza, the bishop of Siguenza. The present castle was built after this leveling took place. The castle of Jadraque (plate no. 21): "Dryness, livid or red land. An abrupt cone of almost vertical slopes—in balance, up on the peak, the aggressive mass defying the surroundings. . . . An enormous presence buried in memory's background! Almost always broken-down, set arrogantly above, the castles have a biting presence. The bare countryside, with the sierra in the background, seems like a skeletal jawbone, where only one tooth remains." If Ortega y Gasset could see it now, he would see that the set of teeth has been rehabilitated with new dentures. The people of Jadraque have restored its castle. A rare case.

Embid (plate no. 15) is a modest fortress built between Aragón and Castile during the reign of Alfonso XI. There is nothing superfluous or ostentatious about this castle. Its walls are made of rough brick topped by simple battlements, devoid of any of those peculiarities that often gave fifteenth-century castles their refinement. Everything is naked and elementary; even its grandiose proportions and great size seem somehow modest. The only outstanding characteristic is its hexagonal enclosure, with large cylindrical towers at each angle, surrounding the principal one.

Traveling from the province of Guadalajara, on to poor and distant Cuenca, one arrives in Moya. Not far from Rincón de Ademuz, in the easternmost section of the province, in lands belonging to the Turia watershed, is seated a castle that was the stronghold of the marquis of Moya. Mutilated, like so many others, its dark stones burn in the sun. It is an example of the inevitable, of the irreversible and fatal, of that which is gone forever. On a small hill in the most deserted part of the Cuenca section of La Mancha—it may not have been so desolate in the fifteenth century—arises one of the most beautiful and original of all fourteenth-century Spanish castles: Belmonte (plate no. 23).

It was constructed in 1456, by the influential lord Don Juan Pacheco, marquis of Villena, steward of Henry IV. Its plan, unique in Spain, is of an equilateral triangle, which forms the parade ground; two of its sides have galleries, and behind them lie the rooms that compose the civil palace; on the third side of the triangle arises the principal tower, the center of the fortifications. All the projecting angles have cylindrical towers with machicolations. As a first line of defense the castle is surrounded by a wall with a parapet walk, staggered battlements and loopholes, and three gates marked by round crenellated towers. The interior must have been extraordinary, a mixture of naturalistic Gothic and *mudéjar*. As proof of its almost decadent refinement, and contrasting with its military style, one of the drawing rooms contained a revolving suit of Gothic-*mudéjar* armor, which by means of colored glass inlays offered surprising plays of light. Its history reminds us of the ill-fated Beltraneja, who was imprisoned there, a sad instrument of the Pacheco ambition.

Such a luxurious and aristocratic building—half fortress, half palace—must have demanded the work of many notable craftsmen, beginning with the designer who conceived it. It is not a typical Spanish castle even though, as is frequently the case, its interiors are adorned with *mudéjar* art.

The castle greatly interested Don Vicente Lampérez, who sketched it and began to restore it for the Empress Eugenia, who would recall her friend

Viollet-le-Duc and his romantic undertaking in rebuilding the castle Pierrefonds. Today it is in ruins, and after an incomplete restoration, it is a sad remain.

The castle of Moya (plate no. 1) in Cuenca occupies a strategic point at the borders of the Kingdoms of Valencia, Castile, and Aragón. Built on the summit of a high ridge and defended by cliffs, it is practically immune to assault.

The eastern side of the enclave, being most vulnerable to attack, is protected by a double wall, while the southern side is protected by the castle itself. A connecting wall, which shows a strong Islamic influence, is attached to this side. The castle is separated from the town by a ditch and a strong wall fortified with cylindrical towers. Inside, at the foot of the principal tower, is a small court of arms.

An extant manuscript lists the privileges granted to the town by the royalty of Castile, from Alfonso VIII to Queen Isabella. The town, granted to the House of Alba, was involved in the disputes of the Carlist fighters who took shelter in this remote place. Today, the town of Moya is practically abandoned and both town and castle have, therefore, preserved much of their medieval ambience.

The province of Albacete was difficult to classify when Spain was organized into autonomous regions. Traditionally Albacete, with the province of Murcia, composed the so-called Kingdom of Murcia or the Murcian Region. But keeping in mind its climate, the nature of its soil and its agriculture, it was added as an extension to the Manchegan Region, leaving Murcia which by itself constitutes an autonomous region.

One of the most beautiful Spanish rock castles is found in Albacete. There are many similar castles but none as daring as that of Almansa (plate no. 10). Above almost vertical cliffs—true walls wrought by nature—there arise as almost a prolongation of these cliffs several walls and a strong principal tower that dominates them all. A castle of the Knights Templar, it continued its eventful history after it was taken over by the crown in 1319. The walls of Almansa witnessed battles, political pacts, meetings of princes, and the memorable battle of 1707, which decided the war between the Bourbons and the Austrians for the Spanish crown.

The Battle of Almansa, the great victory of the duke of Berwick, Jacob Fitz-James, himself major-general of France and general in charge of the Spanish army, took place on the plains at the foot of this castle, one that Fitz-James designated a ''most faithful castle.''

21.   JADRAQUE (Guadalajara)

22. LA CALAHORRA (Granada)

23. BELMONTE (Cuenca)

IN THE LAND OF OAKS

IN no other region in Spain is the landscape so pleasant and peaceful as in Extremadura," according to the celebrated Don José Hernández Pacheco. The count of Canilleros, a famed Extremaduran nobleman, claims that the white peaks of the snow-covered northern mountains bleach the brilliant green of the orchards and gardens below them. As one moves south, he continues, the color of the land is alternately tinted by the gray of granite and ancient olives, the deep green of corks and oaks, the gold of wheat, the red of poppies, the emerald of the vines, and, finally, the deep blues of the sky glowing beyond the horizon.

Northern Extremadura is dominated by chains of mountains, the Gredos, La Vera, Hervás, and Gata, branching off from the main Carpetovetónica range that bisects the peninsula. A second range of mountains to the south cuts across the great plains of the region. The Oretana mountains divide Extremadura into upper and lower halves, corresponding to the provinces of Cáceres and Badajoz. In the central range of the mountains rockrose, thyme, and rosemary adorn the banks of streams, while in the valleys below, oleander and other colorful flowers spring up. Pine, chestnut, walnut, lemon, and palm trees all grow on the land. In some places tropical vegetation can be found just a few miles from snow-covered mountain peaks. But the tree that best characterizes the region, a tree found in many regions of Spain but nowhere so plentifully as in Extremadura, is the evergreen oak.

Upper Extremadura is the more severe land, more rugged and wild. It is more beautiful, no doubt, but also far poorer than the land to the south. Lower Extremadura, sloping toward Andalucía, possesses some of the most productive and fertile country in Spain, including the well-known land of Barros. Lower Andalucía may lack some of the vigor of the north, but agriculturally it is much richer.

Extremadura received its name during the Reconquest, when the territory was contested by the Castilians and Portuguese during their battles against Islam. As frontier land, it received the name *extremo* ("extreme"), and *extrema duri* could be taken to mean "the frontier in the valley of the Duero." In any case, the land was called Extremadura because it was a border territory on the extremes of Christian Spain. The military orders wielded tremendous power in Extremadura, as they did in Toledo. A number of them were actually founded in the area. The Order of Santiago was created in Cáceres in 1170 during the brief occupation of the city by Ferdinand III of León. The Order of Alcántara was established in 1218, in the town of the same name, near the bridge over the river Tagus that may be the boldest and most elegant bridge in the entire Roman Empire. The enormous buildings of the headquarters of the order, the sumptuous Monastery of St. Benedict, still stand in Alcántara.

Given the warlike history of medieval Extremadura, it is no surprise to find castles and fortresses in abundance, including the finest Islamic fortifications in Spain encircling the cities of Cáceres and Badajoz. Cáceres boasts possibly the most complete enclosure of Almohad walls in the peninsula. Towers and castles proliferated in Extremadura during the Middle Ages due to continual wars between powerful families. The Almaraces, Monroyes, and Zúñigas in Plasencia; the Altamiranos, Bejaranos, and Añascos in Trujillo; and the Sabandos, Ulloas, and Golfines in Cáceres littered the region with strongholds like Blasco Muñoz, Valdés, Belvis de Monroy, Almaraz, Albuquerque, Mirabel, Jarandilla, Montánchez, Zafra, Medellín, and others.

Reinhart Wolf photographed only two castles in Extremadura. The first is in Trujillo, city of Pizarro and the most beautiful medieval city in Extremadura. The other, the castle of Nogales (plate no. 24), is in Badajoz.

Trujillo, in the province of Cáceres, is Spain's San Gimignano. Despite the fact that most of its buildings date from the Renaissance and that its best palaces are Plateresque in style, it has more medieval flavor than any city in Spain. The disposition of its buildings is medieval, as are its walls and castle and the towers of its noblemen, some being demolished while others stand proudly. Medieval, too, it might be added, are its famous storks. Riding through the main square of the city with plumed helmet and sheathed sword, Mrs. Huntington's Pizarro is a medieval *caballero* returning from battle like a *condottiere*.

Trujillo is a medieval city, and its castle (plate no. 19) dominates the city from its location atop a ridge. It is a large castle, with sharp angular towers built of fine granite so baked by the sun for centuries that it has a warm, golden hue. A few poor olive trees struggle submissively at its base. It is a castle that looks more like an *alcazaba*. The castle of Trujillo was originally an Arab fortress built on a Roman *castrum*, and later rebuilt a number of times by Christian conquerors. Like so many castles in Spain, it belongs to no single age or architectural style.

In Trujillo, one breathes the air of the conquistadors; Pizarro, Hernán Cortés, Alvarado, Balboa, Valdivia, Orellana, Soto, Belalcázar, and many other famous or forgotten warriors came from the city. In the palaces of Trujillo, which display the arms of the great families and the heraldic emblems granted by Charles V, it seems as though the breathing of these valiant captains can still be heard.

Nogales (plate no. 24) is a fortress built around a large central tower, simple in structure but still an imposing mass. Around the tower is a quadrangular enclosure with cylindrical towers at the four corners and a wide moat. Its clear, elemental design recalls certain structures in northern Spain, such as the tower of the Muñatones in Musques (province of Vizcaya). The castle of Nogales is an elegant construction anticipating the symmetry and harmony of later Renaissance aesthetics. Built by the powerful Suarez family of Figueroa, the building reflected the fine taste of its patrons, who years later commissioned the beautiful Renaissance courtyard in the palace of Zafra.

Wolf photographed Nogales from within a stark landscape of oaks, their thick, leafy branches lightly touched by the golden light that bathes the distant castle. In the words of José Luís Herrera, one of the most knowledgeable writers on the Spanish landscape, the obstinate presence of the oak embodies the very heart of Spain. "The oak is like a cloistered olive tree; a dried, impoverished olive hardened by circumstance."

In the fields of Castile or Extremadura
Always unyielding, always the same,
Impassive, chaste and pure,
Oh, so vigorous and serene
You eternal country oak.

—Machado

Warmed by a strong winter sun, the long-suffering oaks are the eternal companions of the Suarez castle of Figueroa.

IN THE VALLEY OF THE EBRO

ARAGÓN is often identified with ancient Iberia, a land given life by one of the most abundant rivers in the peninsula. The river Ebro crosses Spain diagonally from north to east, originating in the Cantabrian highlands and emptying into the Mediterranean. Aragón follows the course of the Ebro and its tributaries, one of which, the river Aragón, has given its name to the region. It is a land of enormous contrasts: bare desert wastelands and marshy swamplands on the one hand, and on the other, verdant gardens where water runs through narrow river valleys creating oases of perpetual green. These striking contrasts have surely shaped the character of the region's people. The Aragonese are coarse, exuberant, and outgoing. A man like Goya could only have come from Aragón.

Except for verdant strips of garden along its waterways, Aragón is a desolate, irredeemable land; but it is full of its own unique grandeur. As in much of Spain, the geological formations date from the Miocene era. These formations extend throughout both Castiles, the Kingdom of León, and most of La Mancha and the Ebro valley, but nowhere is the Miocene presence as evident as in the deserts and cliffs of Aragón. The land was formed by the evaporation of great tertiary lakes, which left

24.　NOGALES (Badajoz)

25. PEÑAFIEL (Valladolid)

26. LOARRE (Huesca)

behind large deposits of fine loam, marshland, clay, and sand with layers of calcareous tufa on the surface. This layered structure reveals itself at intervals with white veins of pure gypsum. Only miserable brambles and halophytic plants can grow there, and Spain boasts more varieties of such plants than all the other countries of Europe combined.

Don Cristóbal Guitart Aparicio informs us that despite centuries of destruction, Aragón still possesses a great many castles. "We regret all that has been lost, but if we look around at what is left we will find quite a bit more than most people believe. In many places, a castle or grim-looking tower is a living testimony of local history. Whether or not it has any artistic merit, such a building is usually the oldest monument around. The structures that survive are not just crude fortifications guarding minor passes and villages. Aragón boasts fine examples of monumental architecture of all styles: the Romanesque Loarre; the Cistercian Monzón and Sádaba; the Gothic of Mesones, Albalate del Arzobispo, Valderrobres, Mora de Rubielos, and Uncastillo; and the mixed styles of Alquézar, Alcañiz, and Illueca. As for specifically castellated structures, in Biel, Abizanda, and Navardún we find huge Anglo-French dungeon towers. In Calatayud, Daroca, and Albarracín we can find splendid fortified complexes with several castles, gates, and rings of walls wonderfully adapted to the steep and irregular terrain. The citadel of Jaca boasts an almost perfect example of bastioned fortifications, built after artillery came to dominate warfare during the Renaissance. Even royal palaces like the Aljafería in Zaragoza and La Zuda of Huesca were adorned with ostentatious fortifications, and occasionally monasteries too, such as Veruela, were encircled by military walls. The castles of Trasmoz and Boltraña were said to be possessed by witches, while Daroca, the Aljafería, and Sabiñán have their own sentimental legends."

A few castles in Aragón were actually destroyed by war. During the Carlist wars of the nineteenth century, the castles of Segura, Monreal del Campo, Montalbán, Calanda, la Fresnada, and Samper de Calanda all disappeared, while those of Caspe, Alcalá de la Selva, and Castellote suffered irreparable damage. The civil war of 1936–39 destroyed the castle of Siétamo. Yet these buildings were built for war, and to die in such a way is more honorable than by the prosaic pounding of hammers and picks that has destroyed so many others over the years. Those castles that do survive have usually been vacant for centuries, and in many cases they have remained free of the extensions and reconstructions added to buildings of uninterrupted use such as churches, convents, private houses, and public buildings. A few, like Monreal de Ariza, Cervera de la Cañada, Albentosa, and Monterde, serve today as cemeteries. Because of the solidity of their construction, their remote locations, and the centuries that have passed since their occupation, many castles preserve their original structures in pristine condition and can be studied as if they had just been built. A different fate has befallen the walls and towers of urban areas, except in a few cases where specific topographical peculiarities and a lack of expansion have permitted their preservation as in Daroca, Albarracín, Cantavieja, Mosqueruela, Mirambel, Sos, and Ainsa.

* * *

Perhaps the most famous castle in Aragón, noted for its age, extraordinary quality, and spectacular location in the Pyrenean foothills of northern Huesca, is the castle of Loarre (plate no. 26)—prince of Romanesque castles in Spain. It is only one of the many fortress-monasteries in the country, but its beauty, craftsmanship, and rich history are unequaled. Sancho Ramírez, king of Aragón, founded a monastery of Augustinian monks at Loarre in the eleventh century, and construction had begun on the buildings by 1071 when the foundation was sanctioned by Pope Alexander II.

Loarre is a masterpiece of the Jaca Romanesque, an architectural style that spread from La Seo cathedral of Jaca along the pilgrimage roads to Santiago de Compostela. The church has a single nave divided into two bays and a semicircular apse. The square bay before the apse is crowned by a hemispherical dome on double squinches. The monumental proportions of this interior are surprising for an eleventh-century building.

The entire complex sits atop a gigantic rock, one of the last spurs of the Pyrenees, and from its walls we have a panoramic view of the distant horizon of the valley of the river Gallego.

Loarre's handsome complex is dominated by the principal tower and a secondary "tower of the queen," which is the oldest remaining structure in the complex. The crowning achievement, however, is the church attached to the flank of the fortress and which is clearly visible. We enter by way of the crypt through a beautiful Romanesque door with elbowed columns and a checkered archivolt bearing a mutilated inscription that reads: "*Aedes-Has-Municas Invictas—MCIII*" (*Preserve inviolate these houses—1103*). On our modern calendar, that year would be equivalent to the year 1065.

Calatayud (plate no. 11) received its name from the *Kalat* ("castle") de Ayub, named after the emir who first fortified the city. In 1126 it was conquered by the Christians, and during the Middle Ages it became the battleground of Peter IV of Aragón and Peter I of Castile. In Moorish times, the prosperous garden city at the confluence of the Jalón and Jiloca rivers was defended by five castles linked by walls along the heights overlooking the city. Of all those constructions, almost nothing remains today except bricks, mud, and dirt. It is impossible now to tell the difference between the old mud walls and the natural ridges of clay. The work of man resembles nature's and, in its slow destruction, has returned to her.

Mequinenza (plate no. 20) seems minute on its great pedestal, formed of layers of calcareous and argillaceous sediments. The castle appears crystalline and pure, and the edges of its restored towers recall the architectural geometry of Louis Kahn. Only the eastern deserts of Aragón could have produced such an image. Against the horizontal plane of stratified sediments, the ragged wall descending from the castle is just an indentation in the mountain much like the stairs of a gigantic Mexican pyramid.

Pascual Madoz writes about the castle: "It is situated on the top of an isolated mountain that serves as a barrier between the Ebro and Segre rivers which meet at its foot. It is six leagues from Lérida, one from the convent of Escarpe where the Cinca meets the Segre, three from Fraga, nine from Monzón, sixteen from Zaragoza and eleven from Tortosa. It consists of a fortress or old palace of the Marquis of Aitona. . . . It is called *El Macho* and is built exceedingly well. There is a large cistern at its center and it is surrounded by a parapet that in some places nearly touches the central towers while at others is more than five meters away." Madoz goes on to describe the entire defensive system, which must have been extremely complex, and he ends with a lament on the miserable state of the castle today. Such neglect is unfortunate, he says, as the geographic and military importance of the site could make Mequinenza a crossroads between Castile, Navarre, Aragón, Cataluña, and the Mediterranean along the rivers Ebro, Cinca, and Segre.

Sádaba, in the region of Cinco Villas, must have been settled at the end of the eleventh century. In the thirteenth century, when its castle (plate no. 3) was built, it may have served as a defensive base for the kings of Navarre, to whom it belonged for almost half a century. By the beginning of the seventeenth century, the castle had already been abandoned. The Sádaba area is famous among lovers of archaeology for its interesting late-Roman funerary monument built for the Atilios clan.

The castle preserves much of the look of the Moorish fortresses, and it even has something of the *ribats* of North Africa. Although built by Christians, the castle most certainly retains something of earlier Islamic fortifications apparent in its corner portal. It is built on a quadrilateral plan with seven rectangular towers that have semicircular windows and loopholes for archers. The main courtyard contains a Cistercian chapel and the remains of various rooms. Its most striking characteristic is its vertical posture. The ring walls are tall but the erect and unadorned towers are much taller, and their narrow bases give them a heightened elegance.

27.   BERLANGA DE DUERO (Soria)

28. BARCO DE ÁVILA (Ávila)

29.   COCA (Segovia)

BETWEEN MOUNTAIN PEAKS AND OLIVE GROVES

JEAN SERMET wrote in *L'Espagne du Sud*, a book very popular in the 1950s, "At least on the first visit, and sometimes still on the twenty-first, there is no place that can so captivate us, so touch our innermost being, sweep us away on such a wave of delicious and amorous delight as Andalucía." It is a land of disconcerting diversity, a mixture of fertile valleys and rugged highlands where tropical plantations meet the highest mountains in the peninsula, covered all year long with snow.

Between the Sierra Morena and the Cordillera Bética, the broad valley of the Guadalquivir stretches from west to east. It is one of the richest lands in all of the harsh peninsula. A smaller and geographically more complex valley opens on the hidden plain of Granada, surrounded by high mountains that stretch to the shores of the Mediterranean and prevent the development of all but the most modest agriculture. There is also the so-called Andalusian steppe in the old Kingdom of Murcia, one of the poorest and most desolate areas in Spain.

If the plains and mountains of Andalucía are so diverse, so also are her cities. Manuel Machado defined them elegantly:

Cádiz, salty and clear, Granada
Hidden water that it cries.
Roman and Moorish, quiet Córdoba.
Málaga, cantaora.
Almería, bathed in gold.
Silver plated, Jaén.
Huelva, the shore
Of the three caravels
And Sevilla!

The beauties of Sevilla, Córdoba, and Granada may captivate us, but the villages of Andalucía have an inexplicable attraction of their own. "They are high on solitary hills like Salobrena or Arcos de la Frontera, or lost among olive groves; cluster at the edge of the sea like Maro or hide themselves in the mountains. Some affect an aristocratic composure, like Estepa, or a rural disdain like Porcuna or Lopera. They are Renaissance cities such as Ubeda or Baeza with a Castilian flavor or, like Ecija, they stretch out on the plain with a peasant frankness. They have the bashful introspection of Antequera or the modesty and subdued elegance of Carmona. What, then, do these Andalusian villages, so similar and yet so different, have in common? They are as distinct from one another as if they came from different regions, but at the same time they could not be more purely Andalusian. What powerful, vital species begat them and could possibly have raised such a divergent, dynamic breed?" So Julián Marías has identified the mystifying diversity and unity that dominates Andalusian life.

By way of the towns we encounter the castles of Andalucía. Have the castles of Andalucía imprinted the land and history with their majestic and dominating presence? Yes and no. When imagining these warlike monsters, with big, muscular towers and thick growths of trusses, turrets, and gargoyles, as Ortega y Gasset would say, immediately Castile comes to mind, both because of its name and because in Castile the most famous fortresses in Spain's medieval history can be found. But Andalucía has something that Castile does not, and that is the *alcazaba*—beauty of Arabia.

The *alcazaba* is both a castle and a palace, and it is the seat of a court that dominated its town like a powerful lord watching over his domains. *Alcazabas* are often confused with *alcázars*, but there are subtle differences between the two. The special nature of the *alcazaba* can best be understood by reading Emilio García Gómez's inspired essay, ''Alcazabas Moras,'' in his book: *The Throne of the Moor and New Scenes of Andalucía.* ''I am, perhaps, a victim of professional bias, but I confess that of all Spain's admirable monuments I feel a special affection for the Moorish *alcazabas*. They tend to be built of simple mud brick and lack the strong stone fabric of Christian castles. They

stand red or brown between fields lined with olive trees or slopes speckled with almonds set above a quiet river or perched on the edge of a steep precipice. Old, toothless, and worm-eaten, they look like the earth itself molded and made human by history, crowning the most beautiful hills of mountainous Iberia.

''Look at any one of them. You know nothing of its past? It matters little. Imagine a romantic adventure for the place—your hero could be an emir of Córdoba or a bandit of the nineteenth century—or simply delight in its admirable physical presence. Do you know the history of this place is older than the history of these castles? Then you must remember the Roman road that once passed by here. You must know that the castle defended this pass, that it garrisoned that territory; that a caliph built it and an insurgent defended it; that during the war of Granada its governor was killed before the walls and that it is mentioned in a frontier ballad. That if you dug in the courtyard you would find tiny square coins, rusted lamps and bits of old pottery, fragments of those Arabic inscriptions with the tall letters—spikey epigraphic thistles—that create leaves of perennial whiteness in the springlike marble.'' Then the description explodes into a flaming eulogy: ''Moorish *alcazaba*, crown of cities and empress of land and sea, tiny, lonely, peasant castle, guardian and ornament

87

of the lands of southern Spain!''

There is no doubt that the queen of the Spanish *alcazabas* is the Alhambra de Granada, but there are many others: the impressive *alcazaba* of Almería, and those of Alcalá la Real, Málaga, Guadix, Tiñana, Carmona and Utrera, and Alcalá de Guadaira. The Alcázar de Sevilla can also be considered an *alcazaba*, although the urban environment growing up around the building denies it the wild, rustic quality that we associate with Andalusian *alcazabas*. The Moorish *alcazabas* as well as the Christian castles have nourished the romantic image of Andalucía.

To recreate the happy, prosperous world of eighteenth-century Andalucía, one must turn to those villages and small cities that still appear as if they were layed out for a baroque fiesta, or look at one of the groups of farm houses that once dotted the plains and that resemble miniature rural Kremlins surrounded by brick walls and crowned by little towers. The *alcazabas* and castles, on the other hand, give an unmistakable impression of romantic Andalucía as it was recreated by travelers in the nineteenth century. The Andalucía of Washington Irving, Prosper Mérimée, Richard Ford, Gustave Doré, David Roberts, and Théophile Gautier would have as a backdrop a print of the Alhambra or one of the disturbing *torres bermejas*, a castle or *alcazaba* clinging to a giant rock and inhabited by bandits, smugglers, or gypsies. The most thrillingly romantic image of Andalucía is Gustave Doré's print *Une Soirée de l'Antequerela* published in the book *L'Espagne* by Baron de Davillier: In the background the towers of the Alhambra are silhouetted against a dark, sinister sky at dusk.

Romantic images of the Andalusian landscape often include a view of a castle keeping watch over the calm valley of the Guadalquivir from the rugged mountains of Ronda or Algodonales, Grazalema, Priego, Cazorla, Baza, or the Sierra del Viento.

The castle of Vélez Blanco (plate no. 12) in Almería, whose interior once epitomized Renaissance architecture, appears from the outside like a Gothic fortress standing on a rock; it contrasts starkly with the humble whitewashed village below. The ruins of the castle of Olvera in the province of Cádiz, atop its high escarpment, presents the same romantic image as Arcos de la Frontera and Jimena de la Frontera; Belmez in the province of Córdoba; Salobreña in Málaga; Alcaudete, Alcalá la Real, and Segura de la Sierra in Jaén; and many others.

This eagle's nest of the powerful Don Pedro Fajardo, marquis of Vélez, is the best example we have of how a great lord lived at the end of the Middle Ages. The castle of Vélez was at the head

30. LA IRUELA (Jaén)

31. MOLINA DE ARAGÓN (Guadalajara)

32.   ISCAR (Valladolid)

of Fajardo's estates and the seat of his small court. Like La Calahorra (plate no. 22), built by the marquis of Zenete, the castle of Vélez successfully combined a medieval fortress with a Renaissance palace. The courtyard, now installed at The Metropolitan Museum in New York, is the equal of any Renaissance mansion of the fifteenth century.

Except for its combination of medieval and Renaissance architecture, the castle of Vélez has very little in common with La Calahorra. It is built on a high rock, its picturesque irregularity necessitated by the abrupt changes in the land. It looks essentially medieval while La Calahorra is ordered and symmetrical. But both are surprising buildings.

La Calahorra, set against the white backdrop of the snow-covered Sierra Nevada in southeastern Spain, is the finest Renaissance castle in the country, the most original and most important. It was the bold conception of Don Rodrigo de Vivar y Mendoza, first marquis of Zenete, a descendent of the great cardinal, who from birth exhibited both the belligerence of a nobleman of Henry IV's court and the tastes of a Renaissance magnate. This contradictory man, with his anachronistic views, built a similarly contradictory castle: mean and closed on the exterior (already showing the influence of firearms on military architecture) but agreeable and elegant in the interior. La Calahorra is actually an Italian Renaissance palace, the purest one in Spain,

a simple marble courtyard enclosed in a heavy old box. The marquis of Zenete imported a number of notable Italian artisans to help build the palace. They were mainly Ligurians and Lombards, and Michele Carlone seems to have been the most important among them. Construction began around 1509.

The building is a symmetrical rectangle in plan, reinforced at the corners by cylindrical towers. One of these towers is wider than the others. A smaller mass protrudes from one of the long sides of the rectangle containing a suite of rooms built around a beautiful staircase. Reinhart Wolf's photograph brings to mind these lines from García Lorca's *Eulogy for Joanna the Mad*:

> *Granada was your pyre, Dona Juana,*
> *The cypresses your candles.*
> *The sierra, your altarpiece.*

Belalcázar (plate no. 13) is one of Córdoba's most beautiful castles and a typical example of military architecture during the fifteenth century, when seignorial strongholds were at the same time sumptuous palaces. Their warlike exteriors were meant to be intimidating, while their interiors were surprisingly luxurious.

Belalcázar is thirty miles north of Córdoba, in the middle of olive country, which is to say in the middle of Andalucía.

Everywhere we find them.
Thirsty old olives
Under the bright noon sun,
Dusty old olives
On the plains of Andalucía.

—Machado

The sun turns the walls of the castle into gold, contrasting with the green-black beauty of the olives that stretch like a carpet below. The principal tower, rising high above the others, shoots uncrowned into a quiet blue sky. To repeat the words of the poet:

I sing of its elegance with words that whine
And remember a sad breeze through the olives.

The surprisingly well-preserved castle of Almodóvar del Río (plate no. 8) is an imposing mass above the pleasant green meadows of the Guadalquivir. The irregular disposition of its ditches, towers, and enclosures, its shapes and volumes creates an overwhelmingly attractive composition combining rugged strength with great beauty. The castle has been thoroughly and sensitively restored by the marquis of Cubas and the architect Pablo Gutiérrez Moreno, guided by the theories of Viollet-le-Duc. It ended up as a finished specimen of what could be called the personification of the castle aesthetic. Perhaps the marquis of Cubas dreamed of having his own Spanish Pierrefonds, such as the one Viollet-le-Duc restored for Napoleon III and his Andalusian empress, the friend of Prosper Mérimée. Standing as it does now on a rocky ledge overlooking the Guadalquivir, it appears to be more a romantic lithograph than a hostile ruin—like most Spanish castles, a relic of the battle against time.

And, to conclude, La Iruela (plate no. 30). In our catalog of rock castles such as Almansa (plate no. 10), Frías, Vélez Blanco (plate no. 12), Loarre (plate no. 26), Alquézar, and so many others, La Iruela occupies an exceptional place. Seldom has such a steep and inaccessible cliff been converted into a military refuge.

THE book *New York* was a revelation. Not of a photographer —Reinhart Wolf was already one of the world's most prestigious photographers when the book was published in 1981—but of a city. When one has seen the book, New York means much more: pride, refinement, austerity, sophistication, beauty. And it was while he was making the photographs of New York that Wolf conceived the idea of Spanish castles. He tells us: "I think that the men who built the Spanish castles had the same idea as the ones who put up the buildings of New York. Both are manifestations of pride and power. They also have a trace of insanity and madness. It is like a challenge to the gods, to poke and scrape the sky. This is what is behind the skyscrapers, and I think that the building of these enormous castles also expresses a certain madness.

"Another thing I like about the castles is that they have become part of nature, the landscape. They are not protected. It is not like in America where they count every stone that is more than fifty years old. In Spain, a castle is just a part of the landscape, and this fascinates me. I hope it remains this way, especially now that they are putting up fences and barricades to protect them."

Reinhart Wolf is a passionate man, a romantic who feels the emotion of light, and he can transmit these feelings to us by his precise combination of idea and execution. His camera sees what he sees, and his plates reveal his characteristic skill and precision in composition and illumination. But, naturally, each of his photographs is made under different circumstances. Does the film see what the photographer sees? "Like the weather: the sky and clouds are often simply a matter of luck. Knowledge of how film works, however, is professional experi-

ence. During my many years working in publicity, I learned very well the mechanics of photography, because in publicity you get paid for good results. I now know exactly what to expect from the film, years of experience have taught me. I don't think I could have made these photos without my experience in commercial photography. That is why I do not understand those young American photographers who say 'No! we are artists and we will never make commercial photographs. We will only do what we feel, never publicity.' I think this attitude is stupid and banal. It is obviously also absurd to do only publicity even if one is successful. . . . For a long time I worked exclusively in publicity and it was quite frustrating; I was very successful, but it made me feel unhappy and deprived."

The aesthetic range of this affable, friendly, and very, very rigorous man is evident when he tells us: "Yes, I like romantic photographs and the pictorial aspect of photography does interest me. There is one painter, Caspar David Friedrich, who I think has influenced me.

"What interests me about my kind of photography is the combination of spirit and technique. I am a melancholy person, a romantic spirit, and I have a great sensitivity to light; but on the other hand, I am a sure technician, I know how to use filters and lenses, how to do things, but I do not think much about such things. Technique is interesting because it enables me to do what I want; I need it, but it is a small thing—I want to say that, yes, it is a good thing, a necessary thing." But Wolf, unlike many other photographers, achieves his prodigious feats of color without retouching, without any manipulation of the plate.

"When I make a transparency, after I shoot, that's it, you can't add to it. You have to do everything before the shot;

search out the right angle, move around. I make a number of small polaroids from one side, then the other; I move up close and try to get to know the castle as quickly as possible; I am like a hunter. Finally, I decide where I want to place my camera for the shot. Then I think about what light I need for that angle and that perspective. And I wait, hopeful. Sometimes the light happens the way I want it and sometimes it doesn't, but I try to predict it. This is what happened in the photograph of Coca (plate no. 29). The first time I went there was a gray day and I didn't like Coca at all. I thought, 'I cannot photograph it, it isn't attractive, the village is too close, it just makes no sense.' So I didn't take any photographs and I left. I returned a year later. . . ." Wolf made this book over the course of two trips, the first in March of 1981 for two and a half weeks and the second in March of 1982 for four weeks. "I said to myself, 'I need a dark sky and late afternoon light, then it will be precious.' We went three times. The third afternoon the sky was dark and the sun was shining. The moment was perfect.

"After the shot, there is nothing you can do; well, maybe make a duplicate and change the filtering. I don't think it is legitimate to do in color what Atget did in black and white. I think that modern color photography with a good camera should come out exactly as it is shot, one should not have to retouch afterwards. OK, it can be done, but it is not my method, not the way I work. I admire what Atget did, and I think you are right that I have arrived at results similar to Atget's in some of these photos. In black and white, retouching is a lot easier."

Looking at Wolf's camera, one senses how difficult it must be to manage, to carry it to the desired place. One thinks, really, how much of an adventure his work is, more of a safari than a simple hunting trip.

"The wind is a big problem with a large camera. Sometimes I have to climb to the top of a mountain, as in Mequinenza. From below, it doesn't look like much, but when you climb for an hour, on foot, this marvelous backdrop suddenly appears."

Wolf contemplates the photograph and, no doubt, recalls those moments and smiles. He continues:

"With the camera on our backs, we climbed to the top of the mountain. It was very early in the morning. The road was hard and unpaved. The chauffeur waited below and we were up there for twelve hours. Look, the most interesting thing is that second mountain behind the castle (plate no. 20). You can't see it from below, but once you start climbing it appears suddenly.

"It is wonderful to spend an entire day there, contemplating a castle and getting to know it intimately. In this way, I can become part of the landscape, the atmosphere. Sometimes I send the driver and my assistant to buy food so I can stay there alone. This is what I did, for example, with the windmills of Consuegra. It is one of my favorite photographs (plate no. 2). The castle was difficult to photograph because the windmills have been photographed so many times that an uncommon, original photo is truly difficult to make. I spent an entire day there, observing, looking. When my assistant returned, we ate on the steps of this windmill. Marvelous! We ate a wonderful meal. There was not a soul around, not a tourist, not a constable, no one. After searching all day, making small polaroids, I decided: At eight o'clock in the evening I prepared the big camera. It was difficult to know if the sun would come out again or not. From that shooting I have only this single photograph because the sun came out for a moment then disappeared and never came out again.

"So, I arrived in Spain with five suitcases containing all the equipment. I brought an assistant with me. We rented a car and hired a chauffeur who spoke Spanish. I had previously seen a number of books, maps, and paintings of castles. I have a file that I studied every night. I made a plan of work: where we would go first, which castles I thought were worth the effort. . . .

"I had the idea for this book and I went to the magazine *Stern*. I told them, 'I want to do a book on Spanish castles,' and they said 'OK if you've decided to do it, then go ahead,' even though it was frightening for them because they weren't too interested in Spanish castles."

This is no longer the case; they and we feel enriched by this book. We have a new desire to know these castles, to see additional demonstrations of Reinhart Wolf's natural inclination to create something perfect and beautiful.

Wolf is considered one of the finest photographers in Europe. He was born in Berlin in 1930, the son of an architect. He came to the United States on a scholarship from the American State Department and studied psychology, literature, and art history. He later continued his studies in Paris and Hamburg. In 1956, Reinhart Wolf was given the title Master of Photography at the Bavarian State College in Munich. With this appointment, he established his own photography studio in Hamburg. He has been a professor at the College of Design and Fashion in Hamburg and has sat on a number of professional boards. He was founder and president of the German Art Directors Club.

In 1969, he built his *studio-haus* in Hamburg and began his own commer-

cial film production company. He has had one-man shows in Hamburg and Munich and has been invited to participate in conferences for young photographers at a number of universities. In 1969, he began to use an 8 x 10-inch camera to photograph buildings and other historical structures. His *Faces of Buildings*, presented at the 1976 Photokina, won him international fame. It was published under the same title in 1979. On commission from the Polaroid Corporation, Reinhart Wolf traveled through Georgia in 1977 photographing buildings for another documentary series. His editorial work has become fundamental to his work as a photographer.

The magazines *Stern* and *Geo* have both commissioned work from him. During various trips in 1979, Reinhart Wolf photographed the skyscrapers of New York. The spectacular results form the basis of his book *New York*. In the same year, he traveled to Japan to photograph the culinary arts of that country, achieving photographs of great simplicity.

In 1981, he received the gold medal awarded by the German Art Directors Club for his book on New York. In 1982, the book won him the silver medal of the New York Art Directors Club. That same year he also won the gold medals from both the New York and German Art Directors Clubs for his series, *Art That You Can Eat*, on Japanese cooking. He also received the gold medal at the International Book Fair at Leipzig and a prize awarded by the Cultural Alliance of the German Democratic Republic for his book, *Faces of Buildings*, as well as the culture prize awarded by the Society for Photography. This year he received, with *Stern* magazine, two of three gold medals from the German Art Directors Club for the photographs featured in *Castles in Spain*.

—LUIS REVENGA

1. MOYA (Cuenca)

This castle occupies a strategic site at the borders of the kingdoms of Valencia, Castile, and Aragón. It is built on the summit of a high ridge defended by cliffs that make it practically immune to assault.

The eastern side of the enclave, the most vulnerable to attack, is defended by a double wall, while the southern side is protected by the castle itself and a connecting wall that shows a clear Islamic influence. The castle is separated from the town by a ditch and a strong wall fortified with cylindrical towers. Inside, at the foot of the principal tower, is a small court of arms.

An extant manuscript lists the privileges ceded to the town by the kings of Castile from Alfonso VIII to Queen Isabella. The town, having passed to the House of Alba, was involved in the disputes of the Carlist fighters who took shelter in this remote place.

The town of Moya is practically abandoned today, and therefore both the town and the castle preserve their medieval ambience.

2. CONSUEGRA (Toledo)

The fortress of Consuegra rises in the center of a range of hills, dominating the broad Machegan plain and is exposed to the winds that drive the windmills surrounding it.

The fortress of the castle-convent type belongs to the early years of the Reconquest. It was the original seat of the military Order of Saint John of Jerusalem.

It has three enclosures, of which the outer one forms an enormous long bailey to the north ending with a pair of small angular towers. The second enclosure consists of another ring of walls close to the main body of the castle. It is square in plan, although the south side is angular.

The principal fortification, now a pile of ruins, has a strange layout that, except for its large size, is similar to an English "keep."[1] To the south, and completely isolated from the rest, rises the principal tower, which is connected to the castle by a bridge from the second story. On the west side are traces of a chapel that can be dated from the thirteenth century because of some fragments of rib vaulting.

Over the main door there remain two finely wrought coats of arms, of which the lower one, dated 1557, corresponds to the prior Don Hernando Alvarez de Toledo, natural son of the duke of Alba, and the upper one, dated 1679, to Don Juan de Austria, natural son of Philip IV.

---

1. The English call a certain type of castle "keep and bailey." It consists of a strong tower surrounded by a curtain wall. The "castle-tower," with or without a curtain wall, is found in northern Spain. See Fernando Chueca Goitia, *Historia de la Arquitectura Española*, Madrid, 1965, pp. 652–57.

3. SÁDABA (Zaragoza)

The castle of Sádaba is located in the *Cinco Villas* region on the border between Aragón and Navarre, which formed the frontier between Christians and Moslems in the tenth and eleventh centuries. For this reason, a number of castles and fortified churches were built here in those years.

The castle is built on a rocky platform and looks like a work of the early thirteenth century. It has four sides with six rectangular towers armed with semicircular windows and loopholes. The main gate at one corner shows Islamic influence. The court of arms still contains the remains of a Cistercian chapel and some other rooms.

The site must have been first occupied in the eleventh century, and throughout most of the Middle Ages the castle served as a base for Navarrese raids into frontier territory. By the beginning of the seventeenth century the castle was already abandoned.

4. MOMBELTRÁN (Ávila)

In this beautiful place at the foot of the Sierra de Gredos, where the fortresses of the constables of Castile once stood, there stands today the castle of Don Beltrán de la Cueva, favorite of Henry IV and knighted by him with the title duke of Albuquerque. The castle was built in 1461 and its tall, defiant exterior is still intact. It is, to some extent, a castle-palace and must once have had luxurious rooms inside.

It is surrounded by an outer wall with powerful sloping batters, testimony to the advances in military hardware, especially artillery. The castle itself is pentagonal in plan with large cylindrical corner towers crowned by a machicolated gallery and battlements. There is no real principal tower, but one slightly enlarged tower serves the purpose.

It is one of Spain's finest fortresses of the later Gothic period, and it reveals Italian influences.

5. ATIENZA (Guadalajara)

Atienza is a clear example of a rock castle. Built on a tall abutment of rock, the site of earlier Roman and Visigothic fortifications, it acquired great strategic importance when it became an important link in the chain of Moslem defenses along the Duero river in the eleventh century.

The castle was formed of two walled precincts. The upper walls, fairly low, circled the edge of the rock and were reinforced at the south end by a square tower. The second wall took advantage of a lower cliff, cut artificially in places, and formed a narrow circular area extended at the northeast to make a court of arms.

The historical importance of Atienza is underlined by the reference made to it in the *Poem of My Cid* where it is "a very strong rock . . . [that the] Moors have."

Its excellent strategic enclosure retained its importance throughout the Middle Ages after its occupation by the Christians, and during this period the original Islamic fortress received successive additions and alterations. It was from this castle that the muleteers of Atienza liberated Alfonso VIII when as a young boy he was imprisoned by his uncle, Ferdinand II of León.

The only parts of the castle that remain today are the partially restored principal tower, two large cisterns cut into the rock, one of the gates called *Arrebatacapas*, and a few fragments of the outer wall.

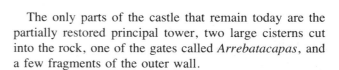

6. PUENTE DEL CONGOSTO (Salamanca)

Fortified bridges were fairly common in medieval Spain, and a few remain such as the one at Frías and those at Toledo.

This one at Congosto, despite the loss of a tower that once rose on one flank, is still defended by a robust and compact castle consisting of a broad, square tower with twin arched windows surrounded by an enclosure formed by a lower wall.

This little fortification, property of the House of Alba, is still well preserved.

7. CASTROGERIZ (Burgos)

On the ridge overlooking the town of Castrogeriz, there remain the ruins of an important but almost destroyed castle that may have Visigothic origins.

The fortification was long and narrow, following the topography of the site. The walls were stout, and a few thick towers, with loopholes for archers, still remain.

The fortress was besieged by the Moslems on a number of occasions during the eleventh century. After six months of fighting, Alfonso VII recovered it from the Aragonese. John II made the town and the castle a county seat and the Supreme Council of Castile resided there during the revolt of the Communeros.

8. ALMODOVAR DEL RÍO (Córdoba)

Almodovar del Río is a grandiose caliphal fortress erected on a high mound along the Guadalquivir. Its high walls are flanked by square towers, except for one that may be Visigothic.

The principal tower is taller than the others, and the entire castle is surrounded by a large moat, while in the middle there is a large court of arms.

During the Almohad invasion, it was the site of an encounter between warring Muslim factions, and Peter the Cruel used it as a prison for his sister-in-law Juana de Lara. It was also the scene of the battles between the followers of Henry IV and his brother. Much later, Philip IV ceded it to the Order of Santiago.

The count of Torralba rebuilt it at the beginning of this century under the direction of the marquis of Cubas, giving it the external appearance of the original Arab fortification. It is one of the few castle-palaces in Andalucía that can still be inhabited.

9. VALENCIA DE DON JUAN (León)

Old Arab mud walls served for the foundation of this fifteenth-century castle in the middle of one of the lordships of the Acuña.

The river Esla protected one of its sides. Four triple towers survive along the southwest walls of the extensive enclosure. The south tower is the principal one, taller than the others, and capped by six thin turrets that protrude from the wall. On the town side there is a ditch defended by a low outer enclosure with thick square towers. The entire work is built of stone.

In the twelfth century the fortress was one of the strongest in León. It was once known as Coyanza until Alfonso VIII gave it the name Valencia. The surname of Don Juan comes from the lordship that the son of Alfonso X held there in the late seventeenth century.

Its present state is one of advanced ruin, despite a number of restorations. The river itself has undermined parts of the walls and has changed from a defensive agent to one of destruction.

10. ALMANSA (Albacete)

The fortress of Almansa originally constituted one of the key Islamic military enclaves, built to reinforce the northern frontier of Arab Spain.

The jutting form of the rock rising from the plain and dominating the town made possible the construction of a rock castle of the *Gran Buque* type—long and narrow to adapt to the terrain.

The principal tower stands out clearly, joined to a narrow platform terminating in two big towers. Another line of walls below, including a large tower with turrets at its corners, completed the defenses at the site.

The Templars were the first to capture Almansa, from whom it later passed to the crown. The castle was besieged by the troops of Henry III during the wars of the Reconquest. During the Wars of Succession in the eighteenth century, Almansa was the scene of Philip V's victory over the Austrian pretender.

The castle has recently been restored and its original battlements have been rebuilt.

11. CALATAYUD (Zaragoza)

Very little remains of the castle of Ayub, which gives the town its name. The town has always been important for its fertile gardens at the confluence of the Jalón and Jiloca rivers.

At one time there were five castles along the ridges that dominate the city; they were connected to each other by long walls. Today there remain only the ruins of the principal castle, higher up on the ridge, and occasional traces of the old walls and a few octagonal and square towers.

12. VÉLEZ BLANCO (Almería)

In 1506, Don Pedro Fajardo, governor of the Kingdom of Murcia, built a castle on the site of the old Moorish fortress of Vélez. His small court resided there amidst the luxury befitting the richest lord in southeastern Spain.

The fortress is a superb example of a seignorial castle. It consists of two separate structures, with a ditch between, joined by two large arches. The smaller building, low and rectangular, has embrasures for artillery. The larger, taller building is hexagonal in shape and has a number of towers, one of which, a rectangular one, is clearly the principal tower. The entire castle, tower and walls alike, is crowned by paired battlements terminating in pyramids and spheres that give a luxurious aspect to the building.

The interior contained at one time a Renaissance courtyard built in Italy of marble, but in 1904 it was sold and transported to a palace outside Paris. It was later acquired by George Blumenthal, who donated it to The Metropolitan Museum in New York where the arcade and staircase with their carved ceiling have been reconstructed outside the library.

13. BELALCÁZAR (Córdoba)

The castle-palace of Belalcázar is one of the most representative of the fifteenth century, when the nobility attempted to demonstrate its social and economic status.

Built entirely of stone blocks, Belalcázar preserves two enclosures: an outer barrier adapted to the irregularities of the land and reinforced with rectangular towers, and the inner rectangular castle-palace with eight towers, one at each corner and another in the center of each side. All eight towers are of average height except for the eastern and principal tower, which rises noticeably above the rest. In the fifteenth century, some Renaissance construction was added to improve the accommodations of the palace, which were insufficient in the old principal tower.

The castle was built by the magnate Gutierre de Sotomayor, grand master of Alcántara, with the benefices he earned from his various possessions. The castle later passed on to the houses of Benavente and Osuna. In 1811, during the War of Independence, French troops defended the castle against a siege by the duke of Wellington's British troops.

The exterior of the fortress is almost entirely intact, but nothing remains of the interior structure.

14. MONTEMAYOR DEL RÍO (Salamanca)

Montemayor del Río was the seat of a lordship, as mentioned in thirteenth-century chronicles. Since its origin, the fortress, on the top of a mountain surrounded by valleys and mountain ranges, seems to have formed a defense against warlike neighbors.

It consists of two enclosures and four towers, including a principal tower of large dimensions. It retains parts of its battlements as well as the main portal, which opens between two short, round towers and originally must have been preceded by a ditch. The entire construction seems to date from before the fifteenth century, given its overall sobriety and the character of its masonry.

Montemayor belonged originally to Alfonso X, who later transferred ownership to his son Don Pedro. Ultimately it became the property of the marquis of Castromonte.

15. EMBID (Guadalajara)

The castle of Embid was a stronghold of the frontier between the kingdoms of Castile and Aragón, not far from the river Piedra.

Its hexagonal plan consists of a wall flanked by towers that recall proto-ogival architecture. The square principal tower is free-standing in the center.

The thirteenth-century document in which Alfonso XI ordered the fortification of this enclave still exists. The castle was later the site of battles between the kingdoms of Peter the Cruel and John II. During the War of Succession it was burned by Austrian troops as they retreated towards Aragón.

The northern part of the building is still intact, including the battlements of the towers and walls.

16. MONASTERIO DE RODILLA (Burgos)

On the medieval frontier of Castile and Navarre there are preserved the remains of a primitive castle whose rocky foundations have resisted the harsh effects of time. It had three square towers to defend three of its sides; the fourth stood at the brink of an inaccessible precipice.

This castle has been mentioned in accounts of battles between the Castilians and Navarrese in the eleventh century, and for some years the Navarrese actually occupied the site. After 1398 the House of Velasco, constable of Castile, possessed the castle and the town.

Nothing remains of its glorious past except for a crumbling line of walls.

17. MONTEALEGRE (Valladolid)

Montealegre formed part of the Leonese defensive line in the twelfth century. Its isolation and its bare, horizontal structure give it the impression of a great fortress.

It has a trapezoidal plan with square towers at the corners and smaller round ones on the walls. The low principal tower is pentagonal. One enters the court of arms through a door with a pointed arch defended by a machicolated gallery above. The building dates to the fourteenth century when the Mediterranean fortification type—small and rectangular with walkways along the battlements, few towers, with the principal one barely differentiated from the rest—began to replace the Romanesque type characterized by a powerful principal tower and a relatively unimportant walled precinct.

The fortress passed through the hands of a number of Castilian families including the Meneses and the Rojas Guzmáns, who in 1626 were each granted the title of marquis of Montealegre.

The exterior structure is in a good state of preservation.

18. GUADAMUR (Toledo)

The castle of Guadamur, in the province of Toledo, is distinctive for its elegant stepped profile. Four progressively elevated elements create this happy result: a low outer barrier, the main body with its towers, a second body with projecting turrets, and the principal tower (on one corner) with its typical turrets projecting on decorated arches similar to the Alcázar de Segovia.

In the main body of the castle, the round corner towers alternate with triangular abutments that look like the breakwaters of a bridge. It seems that the main body of the castle must have been enlarged soon after its original construction since the walls are topped with cantilevered trusses, which in turn support a separate body with entirely different vertical battlements. This extension must have accommodated the palace, and as the castle could not be enlarged beyond its restricted square plan, it was instead extended upwards.

It was built in the latter fifteenth century by Don Pedro López de Ayala, a member of an illustrious Toledan family and much beloved by John II of Castile. Philip the Fair and Princess Joanna spent happy days here on their honeymoon, and Charles V retired here and to the convent of Sisla to mourn the death of Empress Isabella. Cardinal Cisneros also lodged here.

After its days of glory had passed, the castle suffered in the Napoleonic wars and the civil disturbances between the Carlists and liberals, but fortunately it was restored in 1887 by a member of an old Catalan family, the count of Asalto.

19. TRUJILLO (Cáceres)

The Cerro de Cabeza de Toro, or Bull's Head Ridge, was originally the site of a Roman fortification, converted during the Islamic era into an *alcázar* and later rebuilt by Christian conquerors. The result is a group of walls with both round and square towers.

The fortress may have formed part of the great walled precinct that defended the city and was attached to the northeast wall. One passes through a gate into the central area of the *alcazaba*, which has a court of arms and a pair of towers. The towers there are taller than the remaining towers in the castle and may have served as lookouts. To the east are the remains of the *alcázar* with its two marvelous cisterns, one of which has two barrel-vaulted aisles like the one in the Alcazaba de Granada.

The castle was temporarily conquered by Alfonso VIII, and later endured seven consecutive assaults by the Moors and Christians until in 1223 it fell permanently into Castilian hands and became the property of the military orders. In the fifteenth century, Trujillo fought on the side of La Beltraneja, and it was here that the treaty ending those disturbances was signed.

20. MEQUINENZA (Zaragoza)

Mequinenza is located at the confluence of the rivers Segre, Ginco, and Ebro, and since the beginning of the Middle Ages has been an important crossroads in the kingdom of Aragón. It became the possession of the Moncada family shortly after its final conquest in 1141.

The fortress occupies the summit of an isolated mountain. Its plan is an irregular trapezoid with six rectangular towers and one pentagonal tower, none of which protrudes much from the line of the walls. Most of the existing structure dates from the fourteenth and fifteenth centuries, with a few remnants from the thirteenth century, and in the interior some Gothic rooms surrounding a central courtyard are preserved.

Next to the palatial castle there are fortifications built in the early nineteenth century, during the War of Independence, and the military importance of the defenses continued until the War of Liberation. It has recently been restored, and its characteristics as a castle-palace of the late Middle Ages can now be studied.

21. JADRAQUE (Guadalajara)

Arab chronicles mention a castle built here in 801 to protect the valley of the Henares and the access to Guadalajara.

The primitive castle of Sacharaque was demolished by Don Pedro González de Mendoza, at the time bishop of Siguenza, because it was in ruins. Years later, at the end of the fifteenth century, it was rebuilt.

The most impressive feature of the castle is its position on a hill that looks as if it had been created especially for such a castle.

In plan it is a long parallelogram with its sides in a ratio of one to four. There are circular and square towers along its flanks and at the corners. There is neither a principal tower nor a protective ditch, but there is a barbican with strong sloping batters for artillery warfare.

The castle is very sober in profile, with smooth walls terminating in crenellations. It has neither the machicolations nor projecting turrets characteristic of other seignorial castles of the fifteenth century.

22. LA CALAHORRA (Granada)

La Calahorra follows the model of Renaissance castle-palaces: a sober and warlike exterior contrasting with a luxurious interior decorated in Renaissance style. In addition La Calahorra, one of the few castles built by Christians after the fall of Granada in 1492, is built of ashlar instead of the bricks and plaster used by the Moslems.

Built on a slope at some distance from the village, where the Moorish population remained after 1492, it has a rectangular plan with a cylindrical tower at each corner plus a rectangular body extending from the west wall. Its severe exterior, relieved only by barred windows, is built for artillery, and around the castle there is a lower wall, which also has large embrasures for cannon.

The interior is completely different in style, a fine example of Italian architecture brought from that country by Don Rodrigo de Vavar y Mendoza. The main section is a two-story courtyard with arcades on columns, and it was built of 1,200 pieces of marble cut in Italy and assembled in Spain.

La Calahorra is unique not only for its architectural design, but because it is one of the last aristocratic castles in Spain, built at a time when the kings were limiting the powers of the nobility.

23. BELMONTE (Cuenca)

Belmonte is one of Spain's finest castles and was conceived from the beginning as a palace. Its plan is an extraordinary creation. The court of arms, or patio of honor, is a perfect pentagon. Two sides of the pentagon have palatial galleries and facing them is the principal tower, which protects the entrance gate. The major rooms of the palace extend behind the two arcades. The castle is surrounded by a curtain wall with distinct and original battlements. Don Juan Pacheco, marquis of Villena, began building the castle in 1456, and the luxury of its rooms must have been extraordinary. It was partially restored by Don Vicente Lampérez under the aegis of Empress Eugénie, but it was afterwards abandoned and its decay began anew.

24. NOGALES (Badajoz)

The castles of Nogales, Feria, and Zafra (the latter an elegant castle-palace with a remarkable Renaissance courtyard built of marble from Estremoz) formed a defensive system owned by the powerful Suarez family of Figueroa.

Nogales is one of those castles composed of a single large tower surrounded by a ring of defenses, in this case a square enclosure with round towers at the corners. The main tower is much taller than the outer walls, giving an impression of haughty pride. The castle had a ditch around it and a drawbridge that reached the door, which today opens high up on the wall like a large window.

The entire structure is built of fine masonry, and along both the outer wall and the main tower there runs an elegant string of protruding corbels under the battlements.

25. PEÑAFIEL (Valladolid)

Peñafiel is one of the most important fortresses of medieval Castile. The ridge between the Duero and the Duratón rivers must have always been fortified. Count Sancho García conquered the site in the eleventh century, and later Alfonso X left it to his brother, Don Juan Manuel, who undertook important constructions in 1307. The principal tower was rebuilt during the reign of John II. The present structures date mostly from the fifteenth century.

Its irregular plan follows the long, narrow ridge on which it sits. The main walls are very thick and are reinforced by a variety of circular and rectangular towers. A second, lower wall encloses the larger one. The gate is set obliquely into the eastern wall and is defended by two cylindrical towers. From the outer gate one reaches the entrance to the main enclosure by a transverse wall with its own ditch. Federico Bordejé has called this inner gate one of the most perfect in the history of military architecture.

The principal tower dominates the ensemble, and its rectangular form nearly crosses the entire enclosure. Its silhouette is animated by small turrets at the corners and the center of the walls.

26. LOARRE (Huesca)

Sancho Ramírez, king of Aragón, founded a monastery of regular canons at Saint Augustine in Loarre. The foundation was sanctioned by Pope Alexander II in 1071, although construction of the building had commenced before that time. The church has a single nave, divided into two bays and extended by a semicircular apse of almost equal width. The first bay is cut obliquely by the outer wall of the castle. The second bay, in the center of the church, is a full square covered with a cupola. The apse, of course, is covered by a quarter sphere. Because of a sudden drop in the terrain, a crypt was built below the apse. The crypt is a simple semicircular room with a robust blind arcade. One enters it from the middle of a staircase rising from the castle entrance below the church. The entrance to the staircase, and therefore to the entire complex, is an attractive Romanesque portal with elbowed columns and a checked archivolt with a mutilated inscription reading *Aedes-Has-Municas-Invictas*—MCIII ("Preserve Inviolate These Houses —1103"). On our modern calendar that year would be equivalent to 1065. The portal and the crypt must be older than the church, although the form of the crypt pre-figures the structure, which must have grown directly from the same concept. The decorative elements of the portal and the crypt clearly derive from the art of Jaca.

As the church is built over the crypt, the protruding form of the apse rises high above the ground and the bell tower rises even higher. Upon entering the castle the effect is unforgettable. The apse dominates everything, majestic as a rock and carved like a statue. It seems impossible that such a monumental effect could be created in such a steep and enclosed place.

The monastic complex of Loarre possesses, in addition to the chapel/church, a single three-story principal tower and another smaller and more archaic one called the "tower of the queen." This nucleus is protected by a wall that follows the irregular terrain and is reinforced by eight thick towers. There is one entrance to the castle through the tower of the kings, and another through an arched door between two large towers.

27. BERLANGA DE DUERO (Soria)

This castle was built on a long gradual slope cut by a deep ravine. Along with the castles of Gormaz, Osma, and San Esteban, it formed one of the "gateways" to Castile during the medieval period, securing communications along the river Duero.

The present structure is a combination of separate buildings. The first is based on an old Arab fortress, reinforced after the Christian conquest. The square principal tower belongs to this first campaign, although it has later additions. In the sixteenth century, a square palace-fortress was built around this earlier construction, with bulging round towers on the corners containing embrasures for artillery.

Ferdinand I of Castile and Alfonso VI took Berlanga after they conquered Toledo. The area probably remained virtually uninhabited until it was repopulated in the twelfth century, perhaps to prevent an invasion from Aragón. During the time of Don Alvaro de Luna, the region was the scene of fighting between warring bands of nobles. The duke of Frías was given the fortress by Charles V in the sixteenth century, and in 1527 he rebuilt it after damages suffered during the revolt of the *communeros*. He adorned the castle with splendid gardens and an enormous and luxurious interior. The sons of the French king, Francis I, were held hostage here.

The present state of the castle is not very good, although the walls of both enclosures are preserved in a rather mutilated state, as are parts of the wall that enclosed the city.

28. BARCO DE ÁVILA (Ávila)

Watching over one of the principal sheep passages between the upper and lower plateaus, this castle near Alto Torres is an important military fortress.

Parts of the outer walls are preserved largely because they are adapted to the irregularities of the terrain. Inside, the castle itself is square, with four flanking towers at its corners. The main gate, with a semicircular arch, opens onto a court of arms. On its left is the square principal tower, which is connected to the other towers by a walkway. The date of construction is uncertain, although its architecture conforms to the style of the late fifteenth century. The castle was surrounded by two ditches. Both the castle and the outer walls show remains of much earlier constructions.

The castle reached one peak of its glory during the years of the House of Alvarez in Toledo; and another with the dukes of Alba, who expanded and maintained it. The castle and the outer walls suffered serious damage during the Napoleonic wars.

29. COCA (Segovia)

The castle of Coca was built in the late fifteenth century by Don Alonso de Fonseca, one of the most magnificent and luxury-loving magnates of Castile. It lies in the province of Segovia but is close to the border of Valladolid. Cuéllar, Arévalo, Olmedo, and Coca formed a square of great strategic importance.

Built in a sandy, wooded land, poor in stone but rich in *mudéjar* masons, it was naturally built of brick, as were the castles of Arévalo and Medina del Campo, and a multitude of churches in the area. But despite its brick construction, it is not Islamic in plan or disposition. In this respect it is completely Christian. The outer enclosure, with polygonal towers at the corners and semicircular ones on the walls, emerges from a huge moat with views of the artillery defenses. Behind it rise the extremely strong walls of the main part of the castle, which repeat the polygonal and round towers of the outer enclosure. These polygonal forms are especially suited to brick construction.

30. LA IRUELA (Jaén)

The castle of La Iruela is one of the most interesting fortresses of Arab origin in the Kingdom of Jaén, and with its picturesque beauty it is one of the most romantic castles in romantic Andalucía. It is located near Cazorla, in the foothills of the mountain range bearing the same name.

A number of battles were fought here during the Reconquest until Don Rodrigo Jiménez de Rada, archbishop of Toledo, reconquered it in 1231 and made it the seat of his archbishopric.

Its primitive structure is relatively intact. The principal defenses consist of a crumbling principal tower and two separate enclosures, with some of its battlements still intact, connected by a long curtain wall. These walls also protected the monastery, whose remains are still visible nearby.

31. MOLINA DE ARAGÓN (Guadalajara)

Knowledge of the history of the lordship of Molina begins in 1129 when Alfonso I, "*El Batallador*," reconquered the territory. The city and the foundation of the present fortress are certainly much older, however. The celebrated Arab geographer El Rasis in the tenth century described it as an outstanding castle, and in the *Poem of My Cid* it figures as the property of El Cid's Moorish ally Aben Galván.

The lines of the castle reveal its Islamic origin. It occupies the slope of a mountain that dominated the city, and on the high point of the ridge stands the Tower of Aragón, a very tall structure despite the fact that it was cut down during the Carlist wars. The tower is encircled by a small ring of walls and a ditch, and was connected to the rest of the castle by a long wall. The main precinct consists of two parts: a large, walled enclosure and the castle itself built into one corner. The castle originally had six towers, two of which are missing today. Inside them we can still see fragments of the Gothic structure.

Because of its location on the border between Aragón and Castile, it was the scene of frequent battles between these kingdoms. Peter IV of Aragón captured it in 1369 and held it until 1375, when the Castilians recaptured it. In the nineteenth century the fortress was used in the Carlist wars, when some of the defenses were adapted for new types of armaments.

32. ISCAR (Valladolid)

The principal tower is practically all that remains of this fortress, which, although it does contain some older masonry, was almost completely reconstructed in the fifteenth century. The pentagonal tower is itself defended by round and angular towers and topped with powerful machicolations. The fortress was entered through a series of nearly impenetrable doors and stairways. A few towers surrounding it have rectangular embrasures, built for artillery during the sixteenth century.

Iscar was repopulated at the end of the eleventh century by Alfar Fáñez, companion of El Cid, and the castle must have been built to protect the village and the surrounding land. In 1334 it was the scene of a confrontation between King Alfonso XI and his local governor, who refused to let the king enter the castle.

F R A N C E

LA CORUÑA
GIJÓN
SANTANDER
BIARRITZ
BILBAO
PAMPLONA

LEÓN
Monasterio de Rodilla, Burgos (16)
(26) Loarre, Huesca
Valencia de Don Juan, León (9)
Castrogeriz, Burgos (7)
BURGOS
(3) Sádaba, Zaragoza
HUESCA

(17) Montealegre, Valladolid
VALLADOLID
SORIA
ZARAGOZA
BARCELONA
(25) Peñafiel, Valladolid
(27) Berlanga de Duero, Soria
(32) Iscar, Valladolid
(11) Calatayud, Zaragoza
(20) Mequinenza, Zaragoza
PORTO
(5) Atienza, Guadalajara
TARRAGONA
(29) Coca, Segovia
SALAMANCA
(15) Embid, Guadalajara
SEGOVIA
(21) Jadraque, Guadalajara
ÁVILA
GUADALAJARA
(31) Molina de Aragón, Guadalajara
MADRID
BÉJAR
(6) Puente del Congosto, Salamanca
Montemayor del Río, Salamanca (14)
CUENCA
(1) Moya, Cuenca
Barco de Ávila, Ávila (28)
(4) Mombeltrán, Ávila
TOLEDO
(23) Belmonte, Cuenca
(18) Guadamur, Toledo
VALENCIA
(2) Consuegra, Toledo
CÁCERES
(19) Trujillo, Cáceres
S P A I N

LISBON
ALBACETE
(10) Almansa, Albacete
(24) Nogales, Badajoz
BADAJOZ
(13) Belalcázar, Córdoba
ALICANTE

MURCIA
(30) La Iruela, Jaén
CÓRDOBA
JAÉN
(12) Vélez Blanco, Almería
(8) Almodovar del Río, Córdoba
CARTAGENA
SEVILLA
GRANADA
(22) La Calahorra, Granada
JEREZ
MÁLAGA
ALMERÍA
CÁDIZ

N
W — E
S

PORTUGAL

I would like to thank Santiago Saavedra, the publisher of this book in Spain. He not only had an immediate comprehension of the nature of my photographs of the castles in his country, but also took on the publication of this book in Spanish with tremendous enthusiasm and infinite patience.   Reinhart Wolf

The photographs in this book were taken with an 8 x 10-inch Sinar camera with Kodak Ektachrome daylight film. The lenses used range from Super Angulens of 121mm, 165mm, and 210mm focal lengths to Rodenstock Apo-Ronars of 300mm, 480mm, 600mm, and 1,000mm. Polarizing and Kodak color-compensation filters have been used. The apertures most frequently employed were f45, f64, and f90, and shutter speeds varied from one second to several minutes. The photographs have not been retouched or manipulated after exposure.

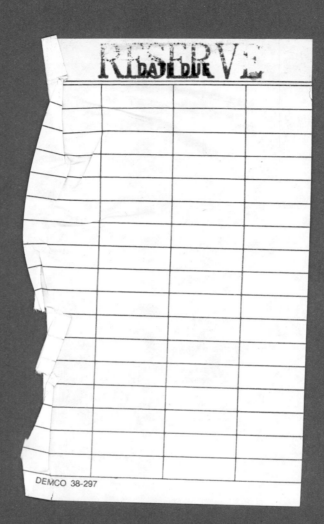

RESERVE

DATE DUE